Diana Bailey.
February 1971.

6/23

£1.-

G000163376

HERTFORDSHIRE

By the same author

The Industrial Archaeology of Hertfordshire
Hertfordshire Inns (two volumes)
Little Guide to Hertfordshire
Companion into Hertfordshire
The Carrington Diary
Welwyn Briefly
Welwyn By and Large
The English Prison Hulks
etc.

1 (overleaf) A village street in Hertfordshire

W. BRANCH JOHNSON
F.S.A., F.R.Hist.S.

HERTFORDSHIRE

B. T. Batsford
London

To STEPHEN the Rover

First published 1970

© W. Branch Johnson 1970

Text printed in great Britain by Northumberland Press Ltd, Gateshead, Co. Durham. Plates printed and books bound by Richard Clay (The Chaucer Press) Ltd, Bungay, Suffolk, for the publishers B. T. Batsford Ltd, 4 Fitzhardinge Street, London W.1

7134 0067 6

CONTENTS

List of Illustrations   8
Map of Hertfordshire   10

          Introduction   13
One   The County and its Roads   15
Two   Before Hertfordshire was Hertfordshire   40
Three   Towns and Villages   58
Four   Castles and the Like   79
Five   Homes Stately and less Stately   107
Six   To the Glory of God   134
Seven   Some Inns   168
Eight   Hertfordshire at Work   197
          Index   219

ILLUSTRATIONS

1. A village street in Hertfordshire   *Frontispiece*
2. Water End, Great Gaddesden   17
3. In Ashridge Park   18
4. Verulamium, the Roman theatre   25
5. In Hemel Hempstead New Town   26
6. A lane at Buckland   35
7. Looking north from near Reed   36
8. Fore Street, Hatfield   41
9. Westmill   42
10. Ashwell, church tower and Mill Street   59
11. St Albans, Fishpool Street   60
12. The Rye House near Hoddesdon   65
13. Hertford Castle   66
14. South front, Hatfield House   75
15. Hatfield House, the Great Hall   76
16. The Main Hall, Moor Park, Rickmansworth   81
17. Ashridge, the chapel   82
18. Tring, the Gore monument   99
19. Hitchin church, market in foreground   100
20. St Paul's Walden, chancel arch   117
21. St Albans Abbey, the nave   118
22. St Albans Abbey from the south-west   135
23. St Albans Abbey, shrine of St Alban   135
24. Sarratt, the saddleback tower   136
25. Detached tower at Standon   136
26. Hemel Hempstead tower and spire   136
27. Stanstead Abbots, St James's Church   136
28. The Bull's Head, Baldock   153
29. St Albans, the White Hart   154
30. The Star at Standon   171
31. New River monument, Chadwell Spring, Hertford   172

32. Milestone, 1732, at Barkway   172
33. Iron bridge, Gadebridge Park, Hemel Hempstead   172
34. Aldbury   189
35. Codicote, the George and Dragon   189
36. Lemsford Mill near Welwyn Garden City   190
37. River Lea at Ware, old malting in background   207
38. On the Grand Union Canal near Boxmoor   208
39. John Perient and his wife Joan (1415), from a brass
    rubbing by R. J. Busby   218

The plates are reproduced by kind permission of the following: Noel Habgood – 10, 30, 34; A. F. Kersting – 3, 16, 18, 20, 22-24; Edwin Smith – 7, 8, 13-15, 21; Jeffery W. Whitelaw – 1, 2, 4-6, 9, 11, 12, 17, 19, 25-29, 35-38.

HERTFORDSHIRE

BUCKINGHAMSHIRE

BEDFORDSHIRE

HERTFORDSHIRE

Pirton

HIT

Hexton

Great
Offle

Lilley

M1

ICKNIELD WAY

A6

DUNSTABLE

LUTON

K
V

Ivinghoe
Beacon

Markyate
St.

HARPEN

AYLESBURY

Flamstead

Lea

Aldbury

Lit.
Gaddesden

Pendley

Redbourn

A6

Wheatha

A41

TRING

Ashridge

Gt.
Gaddesden

M1

Northchurch

BERKHAMSTED

A5

Ver

Boxmoor

HEMEL
HEMPSTEAD

M10

A41

Bovingdon

Kings
Langley

Park
Street

L
C

Abbots
Langley

Co

Flaunden

Hunton Br.

N

Sarratt

Radlett

WATFORD

A41

Chorleywood

Alden

Croxley
Green

Bushey

E

A411

RICKMANSWORTH

A4140

Northwood

Colne

| 0 | 1 | 2 | 3 | 4 | 5 |

Miles

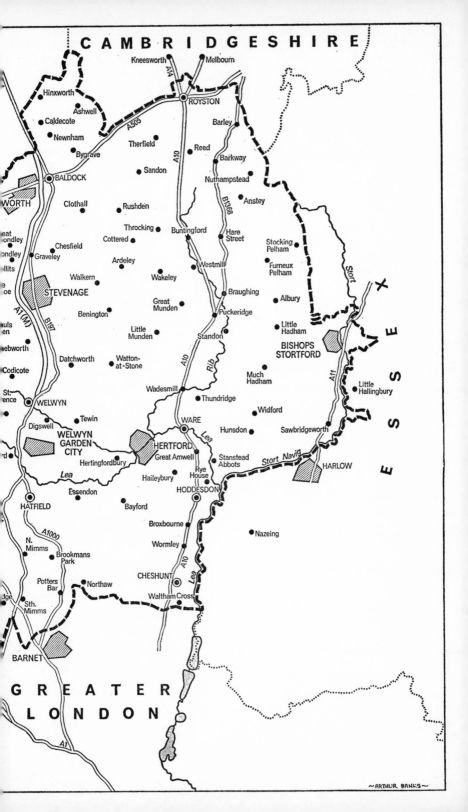

Introduction

Apart from the historic – and quite irresistible – threat of London encroachment, this book has been written under the shadow of two newly arisen ones, both unresolved at the time of its completion.

The first and more immediate is the possibility of London's third airport being established at Nuthampstead, near Barkway, whereby Hertfordshire's remotest and most restful region would be converted into a sprawling town of 50,000 or more people, seldom if ever free from the roar of giant aircraft. In a substantial part of the county, according to the general terms of the Roskill report, 'school windows should be kept shut and some people's sleep [would be] disturbed at night'. Enormously increased road traffic would bring with it inevitable development along the whole length of A 10; and a new branch line of railway to Bishop's Stortford would have to be built. Happily there seem to be technical objections as well to the choice of Nuthampstead – but that choice has still to be made and it is foolish to count one's chickens. Even if Wing in Buckinghamshire were chosen instead, nearly all north Hertfordshire would come within its orbit of objectionable noise. Meanwhile the extension of Luton airport in 1968, and the promise of further extensions in the years immediately ahead, hold out little prospect of tranquillity anywhere, without the gratuitous addition at present threatened.

Shortly after I began writing, the Redcliffe-Maud report on the reorganisation of local government proposed to split the existing county of Hertford between two new unitary authorities. The Hertfordshire of today would cease to be. Here was another facer, upsetting a thousand years of history and shifting old attitudes and old loyalties in who can say what new directions. But some years are likely to pass before the report, no doubt in modified form, is implemented; and obviously nothing that I can do will affect either of these issues.

Towards both therefore I had no alternative but to turn a deaf ear and a blind eye if the book were to be written at all. For its purpose Hertfordshire remains the Hertfordshire I have lived in for approaching half a century, changing vastly in that time, I admit (and still changing), but the same historic county with, as to much of it at least, the same fundamental charm, not wholly disturbed even by the ubiquitous motor car. The only concession to recent events that I have made is the omission of Barnet, which became part of the Greater London borough of that name in 1965, and the inclusion of Potters Bar, formerly in Middlesex, which it received in exchange.

Chiefly for my own peace of mind I would emphasise that mention of any building or other site in these pages does not imply right of public entry. Readers will please pursue their own tactful inquiries on that score. What makes me anxious to drive the point home is that just as I was drafting the last pages of the book the owner of an interesting house in Hertfordshire told me that all through the summer he had been pestered by strangers demanding to see for themselves the things they had read about in a magazine. If he gave them and the magazine writer the rough side of his quite adequate tongue (as I gather he did) he can scarcely be blamed.

A book of this kind is not expected to embody new research and only here and there have I introduced a few items of my own recent discovery. My grateful thanks are due to Dr Ilid E. Anthony, until recently Director of the Verulamium Museum, St Albans, for her approval of my chapter on archaeology; to the county's many local historians past and present, whom I have consulted either personally or through their printed work; to Mr R. J. Busby for advice on monumental brasses; and not least to Mr Peter Walne, County Archivist, and my old friends at the County Record Office.

CHAPTER ONE

The County
and its Roads

Sixty years ago E. M. Forster in *Howards End* described the quiet unobtrusive Hertfordshire landscape, none more than 40 miles from the City of London, as 'England meditative'. Parts of it – a good deal more than is generally recognised – are in their degree meditative still; but nowadays meditation is broken into by agencies of which Forster knew little or nothing – the always intrusive motor-car, the scarifying aeroplane, the soaring pylon and radio mast, the disfiguring domestic T.V. aerial, to say nothing of the transistor carried hither and thither by the younger generation of countrymen. We of today are in process of becoming reconciled to such things, finding less and less difficulty in accepting them as inseparable from the countryside's promise of peace, quietude and refuge from fret. All things, we say, are relative; yet I will make bold to claim that there are moments in Hertfordshire – not many perhaps, but some – when the relative approaches the modern absolute.

The truth is, of course, that it was not by any means all meditative when Forster wrote, even though it remained the least urbanised, the least 'developed', of the Home Counties; bird-song and the cry of the ploughman to his horses were still to be heard in most of it. But London encroachment – one of the major factors throughout its history – was gathering force for a new and massive assault. Today much of the county's southern half is given over to industry and more to the housing of a population trebled in three-quarters of a century and still rapidly rising. Three big self-contained New Towns have appeared in it, with a fourth just over its eastern boundary; old towns have enlarged and modernised themselves; villages have swollen and even the remotest ones suffered invasion, as witness the fantastic price of house property in them. But to bewail the passing of time is among the most futile of occupations. Things are as they are. Willy nilly one accepts them, even though – as in the destruction, sometimes wanton, of fine old buildings – with a sigh of angry resignation, and rejoices in the much that remains, including the, at first glance, unsightly. Why, for instance, gird at a huge recently built malthouse of quite untraditional design at Ware, when it is the modern representative of Hertfordshire's oldest industry, going back to at least the Middle Ages? – or at an immense papermaking factory near Hemel Hempstead, when paper was being made in the county 500 years ago? – or at a large hosiery mill at Baldock, when it is the descendant of a silk industry known in Hertfordshire for at least two centuries? Even the new yellow gravel digging areas in the south of the county might, with some stretch of imagination, be seen as successors to the chalk pits (known as chalkdells) found in countless fields, from which underlying chalk used to be dug by farmers for marling the heavy surface clay. To the discerning the past is apt to live on in unexpected guises; and when all is said, 65 per cent of the county's total acreage is still devoted to the oldest of all industries, agriculture.

What is undeniably fortunate for Hertfordshire is that it contains neither coal nor mineral deposits and that all its rivers are small ones; it has been spared the establishment of heavy industry, that assassin of all natural beauty. Moreover, speaking generally, industry is concentrated into well-defined areas – the New Towns, the Lea Valley, St Albans and, above all, the Watford region, with a smaller concentration at Boreham Wood in the extreme south. Letchworth is the main representative of industry in the north. Residential expansion is less concentrated but on the whole follows industrial; north of a line from Bishop's Stortford through Stevenage to Hemel Hempstead the bulk of the county is almost completely rural, though with considerable rural or semi-rural areas to the south of it also. Main thoroughfares, augmented in recent years by such newcomers as M 1 and A 1 (M), give nowadays no time to stand and stare; but in between them is a spider's web of lanes, narrow, twisting, undu-

2   *Water End, Great Gaddesden*

lating, altogether charming, that are one of the county's more priceless relics of the past, little as the motorist-in-a-hurry may appreciate them. It is understood to be the present policy of the Hertfordshire County Council to preserve in decency as many of these lanes as possible, modernising only the relatively few that serve as busy cross-country traffic arteries.

Round the north and west of Hertfordshire sweep the chalky Chiltern hills, from Royston, by Luton and Dunstable in Bedfordshire, to Tring and on into Buckinghamshire – their highest point hereabouts, Ivinghoe Beacon (811 feet), lies, however, just outside the county. With downland crests giving magnificent views northwards (as on Dunstable Downs, near Reed and again on Royston Heath), hillsides (particularly round Ashridge and the Gaddesdens) richly clothed in beech and oak, and steep lush valleys full of promised peace, they provide the most striking scenery that the county can boast. Much is exhilarating; but to me at any rate not all gives what I want. In west Hertfordshire this Chiltern area includes Watford, the county's largest industrial town, the big New Town of Hemel Hempstead, the choice residential districts of Berkhamsted, Rickmansworth with Moor Park and Chorleywood, and 'posh' villages like King's Langley and Little Gaddesden. No, exhilarating it may be, and is; yet when even at its best I am nagged by the no doubt exaggerated feeling that a new 'period' residence with garage for two or more cars, or a row of eighteenth-century cottages turned into a 'picturesque' executive-type house (built-in garage) may just possibly be round any corner. One or two would, of course, be excusable in such lovely surroundings; more, however thinly spread, make a crowd.

Hertfordshire's eastern and central areas (mostly heavy clay on top of the chalk) are quieter, akin rather to the domestic than the dramatic, pleasantly undulating, cut for the most part into smallish fields of wheat, barley or pasture, diversified by many oak woods, hornbeam copses and tree-lined hedges, containing some of the most picturesque villages as well as the remotest corners of the county. With the exception of Stevenage its towns are small and lie on the fringe, leaving its heart immaculate. This, rather than the

3   *In Ashridge Park*

Chilterns, is, to me, a real honest-to-goodness countryside, less immediately striking no doubt, but slowly seeping into one's consciousness and in the end captivating it – a countryside unsophisticated, intimate yet extraordinarily powerful in its ultimate impact, the attainment of quietude and peace. In a word, still, relatively at any rate, Forster's 'England meditative' – and it was herein that 60 years ago Forster lived.

In the south of the county the countryside flattens somewhat, though it is not uniformly flat. It is a curious mixture – a hotch-potch of new residential areas and new industries, of one or two genuinely rural villages, of thronged and fume-ridden highways, of atrociously ugly gravel diggings and of pockets that perhaps may be described as relatively virgin. Speaking for the whole area, its truly rural character exists to large extent in name rather than in fact; but it is still worth exploration, if only to realise the immense acreage of green (sometimes grey-green) land that survives precariously in the very threshold of Cobbett's Great Wen.

Throughout all these countrysides are villages of every sort, varying from small clusters of cottages, huddled together or rimming a green and far from a highway, to others that have become mere residential overspills to adjacent urban centres. Yet in most of them their churches, almost always in good repair and surrounded by a well-kept churchyard, give a comforting sense of being part and parcel of their town or village, not dominating but sharing it.

On the other hand, apart from St Albans Abbey, Hertfordshire contains little that is famous in ecclesiastical architecture. Perhaps the most impressive examples are the fine Norman church at Hemel Hempstead, the Decorated one at Ashwell and the largely Perpendicular ones at Baldock, Berkhamsted, Hitchin and Watford. Which is, of course, far from saying that the rest do not merit close examination, both for their fabrics and for such adjuncts as brasses, in which the county is rich; or wall paintings at St Albans Abbey, Cottered, Newnham, Sarratt (very faded) and elsewhere; or bench ends and other woodwork at Anstey, Bishop's Stortford, Much Hadham and Sawbridgeworth. The church at Ashwell is well known for the graffiti it contains; less known are those at Stevenage and

Graveley. Very characteristic of Hertfordshire churches is the quaint spirelet, usually known as the Hertfordshire spike, surmounting their towers – there are specially fine ones at Ashwell and Baldock. In general, Victorian restoration dealt more mercifully with churches here than in many other counties – more mercifully, for instance, than recent work at Digswell, where enlargement, admittedly necessary owing to greatly increased population, has been so carried out that, to my mind at least, the dignity and grace of the old fabric is gravely impaired. And even more recently, certain churches in the New Towns appear to have been erected less to the glory of God than as demonstration of the architect's perverse ingenuity – though I will admit that the necessity of having to work on a shoe-string budget with prefabricated materials may at times provide him with a plausible excuse. So too may a widespread search after some new approach to religious expression. But religion, not the architect, must prevail.

Since most people these days are motorists it will be well to consider the county mainly from the motorist's point of view, at the same time reminding him that the car is a stultifying as well as a liberating mode of exploration – not only of Hertfordshire is it true that some of the choicest spots are open to the walker alone. And I may, perhaps, be allowed to emphasise also that the motorist who jibs at the lanes I have just mentioned does himself no service – by jibbing he will lose a great deal of the county's intriguing individuality, its intimate mingling of rural past and sophisticated present within a few miles of territory. All he needs to remember in travelling them – and never forget – is that discretion in speed is the better part of valour. Even with an Ordnance Survey map to direct and a few road signs to give preliminary warning, discretion in speed will rob sudden tree-obscured corners, small unexpected junctions and crossings and sometimes a deceptively empty stretch of their various perils. I remember a 70-year-old Hertfordshire-born motorist, who had lived in the county throughout his life, saying to me, 'I always take these lanes as though each time was the first'.

It may perhaps be found interesting to link up Hertfordshire's roads and lanes with the history of the county, even though it will be obvious that what the motorist – or cyclist or walker, of course – travels today bears no relation whatever to their original state and sometimes little even to their original route.

By far the oldest is the road (A 505) by Royston, Baldock, Letch worth and Ickleford (where it becomes a mere cart track), through Dunstable in Bedfordshire, crossing the finger of west Hertfordshire that contains Tring (B 487) and finally (so far as we are concerned) entering Buckinghamshire. Known as the Icknield Way, it came into existence as a vaguely defined track used by the Neolithic and Bronze Age peoples of up to about 4,000 years ago, following mainly the Chiltern crest above the thick wild-animal-haunted forests that covered the Hertfordshire region. Near it may be seen some of the county's oldest man-made survivals – a long barrow and several round barrows on Royston Heath; Iron Age forts (2,000 and more years old) at Ashwell, Letchworth and Hexton; Iron Age, perhaps Bronge Age, settlement sites on several of the hilltops between Dunstable and Tring and beyond. A little north of Lilley what appears to be an east–west ride through woodland marks the route of this ancient Way, while close by, at Gallows Hill just inside Bedfordshire, is an Iron Age settlement; and there is some reason to believe that a deviation of it, perhaps used in summer only, ran through or very near to Pirton.

These Iron Age settlements were, for the most part, the work of a Celtic people, the Belgae from northern France, who invaded Kent and the Thames estuary probably about 20 years before Caesar's first exploratory raid in 54 B.C. – by which time they had pretty thoroughly established themselves in southern Hertfordshire, with a tribal capital at Marford, near Wheathamstead (parts of its bound ary ditch can still be seen), another settlement at Gatesbury, near Braughing, and smaller occupation sites, mostly in or near river valleys, scattered about a wide area. A fierce, aggressive and, one imagines, an unlovable people, they defied the heavily forested countryside, to spread later over the rest of Hertfordshire and into the counties north of it – only in time to be seduced by the fleshpots of Roman civilisation and absorbed body and soul into it. Their various settlements, when not already linked by the much older

Icknield Way, were joined by rough tracks, some of which were afterwards followed and improved by the Romans, to whom, indeed, Hertfordshire owes virtually all its basic road structure.

There were two principal Roman centres in the region – Verulamium, near St Albans (which we shall visit in the next chapter), and Braughing, about which little is known. From each of these centres roads punctuated the forest; the two, however, which are of the greatest significance are those linking the centre with London – first, generally known as Ermine Street, through Cheshunt, Ware, Braughing, Buntingford and Royston (A 10 to Royston, A 14 beyond) on its way to Lincoln and the great northern capital, York; second, Watling Street, through Elstree, Verulamium, Redbourn and Dunstable in Bedfordshire (A 5) on its way to Chester. From Verulamium ran a road by Nash Mills, near Hemel Hempstead, Berkhamsted, Tring, and Aylesbury in Buckinghamshire to Cirencester and the West, which was joined at Nash Mills by a lesser road from London; in later centuries this became an important London–West of England highway known as Akeman Street and is now A 4141 between London and Hunton Bridge, north of Watford, and A 41 thereafter. A typical fragment of a cross-country Roman road runs from Bishop's Stortford to Braughing (in part A 120); originally it continued to Baldock, where it joined another road into Bedfordshire, but today survives only as disjointed lengths of green lane or cart track between Braughing and Hare Street and again near Clothall. More sections of quiet country lanes may probably be of Roman origin than it would be wise to dogmatise about – but be cautious in accepting the common theory that any straight line of route must be of Roman workmanship; it is quite likely to date from only the Enclosure period of the eighteenth or nineteenth centuries.

A glance at the map will show that the three main thoroughfares mentioned above – A 10, A 5, A 4141 – emerge from London like the ribs of a fan. What of the fourth, the Great North Road through Barnet, Hatfield, Welwyn, Stevenage and Baldock, classified in its various Hertfordshire stretches as A 1000, A 1, and B 197?

In Roman days, throughout the Middle Ages and Elizabethan period and into Stuart times, the only through-route to York and the

North lay along A 10. But it passed by the great malting town of Ware, to which from, at latest, medieval days barley was carried down it by packhorse or wagon from all over the Eastern Counties; with the result that by the early seventeenth century one of England's most important thoroughfares had become unusable. Travellers therefore began to deviate from it at Alconbury in Huntingdonshire, taking a series of lesser roads (some of Roman origin) through Eaton Socon, Sandy and Biggleswade, all in Bedfordshire, and entering Hertfordshire at Baldock. The popularity of this new route grew quickly – Pepys, for instance, was using it in the 1660s and a Welwyn document of that date could speak of the village as lying on 'the great road to London'. Yet no modern traveller would have dreamed of taking it; even to Daniel Defoe in the 1720s it was 'a frightful way'. In 1684, for instance, the people of Welwyn were in trouble for not keeping it eight feet wide (that is, eight feet free from overhanging trees, intruding buildings and other obstacles) and, again near Welwyn, a sharp turn close to a narrow wooded defile made a notoriously happy hunting ground for highwaymen. Highwaymen loved every mile of the Great North Road.

So far as it is possible to generalise, it may perhaps be said that Roman civilisation was fundamentally an urban one, in that its love of organisation tended to create towns, sometimes large, from which administration was carried on over the surrounding region; as in today also, the prime function of agriculture was to feed the town. In southern Britain London soon became pre-eminent as a port; in Hertfordshire, as has been said, Verulamium was the regional hub, with Braughing as possibly a secondary one. Again generally speaking, rural population tended to distribute itself within easy reach of the roads radiating from those centres and along one or two open river valleys, leaving the intervening forest still unexplored. But with Roman withdrawal from Britain during the fifth century a change came over the scene. Saxon bands from across the North Sea, at first merely raiding, later settling, were – and to some extent remained – basically tribal and certainly agricultural in their social structure. The earliest comers to Hertfordshire probably filtered in from the open lands of Essex – the name of Tewin, for instance,

the settlement of the people of Tew (a pagan war-god commemorated in 'Tuesday') suggests the establishment of probably a family farm there before Saxon conversion to Christianity in the sixth century. Similarly Braughing (though not on the site of the abandoned Roman town) is the 'ing', or settlement, of the people of Brahha. An early Saxon hut has been excavated at Stevenage. There are traces of Saxon work in the churches of Reed and Westmill. All down the eastern side of the county we find evidence of fairly early Saxon occupation.

Just when they began to use the Icknield Way as, so to speak, an invasion route is conjectural; their first explorations from it were northwards into Bedfordshire. Only later – say, in the eighth and ninth centuries – did they begin tentatively to penetrate southwards through the dense forest of mid- and west Hertfordshire. Here and there a natural clearing, good soil, an assured water supply or some other advantage led to the founding of, at first, a single farm, a hardy pioneer with the odds of survival against it. If it throve, enlarging its buildings and its cultivation, it would in time be joined, either for defence or for sociability (perhaps for both), by others nearby. Thus, probably, gradually arose a good many Hertfordshire villages, represented by the original farm, surrounded by what are now called Ends and Greens, the later arrivals. And thus arose too the beginning of the network of pathways and lanes – communication between one farm and another, between one settlement and another – that was to develop in later centuries into the spider's web we know today.

But several centuries of Saxon occupation saw more than a purely struggling agricultural community. It was the Saxon king, Offa (said to have had a palace at Offley, though no evidence of it has come to light), who established the present St Albans Abbey in 793; a Saxon town grew up opposite the crumbling walls of Roman Verulamium, and Saxon Abbots founded the three churches of St Michael's, St Peter's and St Stephen's. In 912 Edward the Elder established two fortresses across the Lea, round which the town and borough of Hertford soon clustered. Hitchin, Hatfield, Hemel Hempstead, Berkhamsted, Ware and other towns emerged under Saxon rule, even though some may have seen Roman occupation of one kind or another. But in spite of such tiny pockets of urban development and a number of even tinier villages, it was still forest that dominated the countryside – forest retreating, if only by an acre or two at a time, before agriculture, threaded by a few Roman roads still in tolerable though deteriorating condition and by a growing tangle of lanes – tracks, rather – usable by man or beast in the best weather only.

The social life of all historical epochs is to some extent conditioned by the roads that served it. Those of the Saxons were and remained primitive to a degree that would have shocked their Roman predecessors. The Normans, who followed, did nothing to improve them; and thus there grew up in the minds of people in the Middle Ages a concept of the road not as physical entity but as a right of passage. An example may make this plain.

From A to B there exists a track of sorts – always has done. On its way it takes in a farmhouse here, angles the corner of a field there, crosses a ford elsewhere. Then, at some point or other along its route, a tree is felled by lightning – or a new house is built – or a farmer chooses to dig a chalk-pit or raise a dung-heap; in all cases blocking the road. Such travellers as use it, on foot or by horse, grumble for a time – but not seriously, since they have the right to avoid the obstacle merely by making a new way round it, with nobody to deny them. In a word, to an already winding track has been added another twist – and so, theoretically at least, *ad infinitum*. Chesterton's reeling but endearing English drunkard dissolves into something much more humdrum – a legal concept.

Served by such roads, with little encouragement to improve means of transport and, for many of the 'lower orders', express prohibition on leaving the manor in which they lived, the bulk of people in the Middle Ages were virtually static, except, perhaps, to sell their produce in a nearby market – only the great or the in some way privileged could travel freely, and then with an infinitude of labour, discomfort and danger. In Hertfordshire, however, a further impediment to travel – the agelong forest – was steadily overcome, as arable cultivation expanded to meet the needs of a bigger and still rising population, as an army of free-ranging pigs annually consumed beech mast and acorns, and as timber for house building, charcoal firing and a host of other uses constantly increased in demand. Yet even so, one of the terms on which the manor of Flamstead was granted to its lord was that of protecting travellers from the attacks of highway robbers – a provision very similar to the contemporary appointment in adjacent Buckinghamshire of a Steward to suppress robbery in the Chiltern Hundreds.

It was the Tudor and Elizabethan ages that saw – in spite of little road improvement – a perceptible rise in the popularity of travel, as men's minds freed themselves from medieval restrictions hitherto accepted by them. To such improvement as there was the Government did contribute an important Act of 1555, which imposed upon every parish the duty of paying at least a modicum of attention to its roads; and in 1598 two Roman roads passing through Hertfordshire – A 10 and A 5 – saw the first post-boys carrying official and other despatches from London to the North and halting along A 10 at Cheshunt, Ware and Royston, along A 5 at St Albans. Broadwheeled coaches, heavy, clumsy and destructive, lumbered to and fro; horsemen took to the road for other journeys than the most essential; not only pack-horses but also droves of cattle, sheep and miscellaneous livestock crowded them on their way from market to market or from farm to London. And as accompaniment to all this came, of course, a new era of prosperity to inns everywhere in the county.

Some of those inns were even then ancient so far as their licences were concerned, though all have since been wholly or in part rebuilt. Thus there was an alehouse, kept by Laurence the Taverner, on the site of the *George and Dragon* at Codicote in 1279 and of the *Wellington* (formerly the *Swan*) at Welwyn in 1352. At Bishop's Stortford there was a *George* in 1417; in Hertford the *Salisbury Arms* was the *Bell* in 1431. In the next three-quarters of a century we hear at St Albans of the *Fleur de Lys*, the *Queen's*, the *Cock*, the *Peahen*, the *Bell* and the *King Harry*; and only a few years later of the *George* at Harpenden, the *Star* at Ware, the *Bull* at Broxbourne, the *Rose and Crown* at Hemel Hempstead, the *Salisbury Arms* (formerly the *Star*) at Hoddesdon and the *Bull* at Berkhamsted.

Almost imperceptibly, then, improvement in the roads took place

– and here is one more, and historically significant, confirmation of it. On the dissolution of St Albans Abbey in 1539 all its Hertford-shire manors and estates (and there was a fair number) were acquired by Henry VIII's courtiers and servants. Though Henry loved Hert-fordshire and spent a good deal of time in it, he spent more in and about London; and since attendance on the sovereign was both pro-fessionally required and politically expedient, London must have been more or less accessible to Hertfordshire's new lords of the manor. By Elizabethan times high officers of state – Lord Burghley and Sir Nicholas Bacon, for example, to say nothing of Lords Chief Justice and the like – could reside in it, using its roads, if not with comfort, at least with some degree of assurance. Into the county too came leading London merchants anxious to play the country squire in their leisure moments, though it was only half a century later, in the years following the Civil War of the mid-seventeenth century, that they finally ousted the remaining medieval county families, whose Royalist loyalty, crippling at the time, received no grateful recompense from later Stuarts. Merchants of all kinds, bankers, brewers, lawyers and surgeons flowed into the vacuum created by their downfall; and since to the newcomers London was where they made their money, Hertfordshire where they spent it, a reasonable channel of communication between the two was essential. Indeed, it was for such newcomers, who 'would know the Privileges belong-ing to their several Manors', that Sir Henry Chauncy, the first county historian, compiled his *Historical Antiquities of Hertfordshire* in 1700. Having learned them – and it being, of course, necessary, then as now, to keep up with the Joneses – they set about rebuilding their country houses and remodelling their country estates; with the result that Hertfordshire today is rich in eighteenth-century domestic architecture.

But what, it may be asked, were the Hertfordshire roads – that is, of course, the great highways – really like at that period? That they were narrow, winding, freely impeded, unsurfaced, undrained and liberally pot-holed goes without saying; yet there were con-temporaries who saw little wrong in them. One was John Norden, Queen Elizabeth's Surveyor-General, in 1598: 'It is much benefited by thoroughfares to and from London northwards, and that maketh the markets to be the better furnished with such necessaries as are required.' Another was John Taylor, often called the Water Poet, in 1636, who waxed enthusiastic about the county's 'good clean highways' and 'conscionable short miles'.

Less than 30 years after Taylor wrote, in 1663, an Act was passed putting the upkeep of what is now A 10 and part of A 14 into the hands of the Justices of Hertfordshire, Cambridgeshire and Huntingdonshire; its Preamble speaks of the road as 'very dangerous to all His Majesty's liege people that pass that way' – indeed, as we saw some pages back, it was the shocking state of the road that gave rise to the popularity of its alternative route, the Great North Road. The Preambles of all later Acts creating Turnpike Trusts along main thoroughfares spoke of those thoroughfares as 'dangerous', 'in great decay', 'ruinous', and so on. Norden and Taylor may have been honest observers if one could discover by what yardstick they made their assessments; quite apart from the minatory Preambles (which admittedly had to justify the Acts that followed), Turnpike Acts themselves emphasised awareness of the need for improvement. Both a rising population and an expanding national economy made the need urgent.

By the middle of the eighteenth century all major roads in Hertfordshire were controlled by Turnpike Trusts, paying for maintenance and amelioration out of tolls levied upon users. Some Trusts were prosperous, others remained on the edge of insolvency; nevertheless, to examine the records of any Trust is to watch the gradual straightening of awkward corners, easing of gradients, widening and better surfacing of one road after another – work carried out by Surveyors who were always amateurs and occasionally only part-time employees of the Trust they worked for. Not until the early nineteenth century did the advent of two giants – Thomas Telford and John Loudon McAdam – combined with more skilful coach design and the better breeding of horses effect a revolution in both the speed and the comfort of travel. In remodelling the Holyhead Road round about 1820 Telford built the embanked approach to Barnet from London and substituted the present A 1081

to St Albans for a roundabout route through Kitt's End. In the following years a Government project (finally abandoned) for a similar
remodelling of the Great North Road led to his surveying a Baldock
bypass on almost exactly the line of the present one nearly a century and a half later. Many of McAdam's early experiments in the
type of surfacing that bears his name were made in Hertfordshire,
where he became in the end Surveyor to most of its Turnpike
Trusts (he lived for the last ten years of his life at Hoddesdon) – an
immense responsibility when it is remembered that every coach
from London to the North and North-west passed through the
county.

One Hertfordshire Trust has a curious story. In the early eighteenth century, it is said, the Earl (as he was then) of Salisbury
at Hatfield and the Earl of Essex, who lived at Cassiobury,
Watford, combined to construct and maintain a road from Hatfield,
through Watford to Reading, where it joined the already existing
road to Bath; by so doing they would avoid uncomfortable journeys
to London on their way to drink the waters and follow the fashion.
How much truth lies in this story is not known; but certainly a
Trust was established along the road in 1757. It continued in existence until 1869 and is today recalled in Hertfordshire by its series
of cast-iron mile stones erected in 1822. Sometimes known as Lord
Salisbury's Gout Track, it is now A 414 to St Albans, then A 412
through Watford to Rickmansworth, then A 404 through Chorleywood to beyond the county boundary.

Other factors besides the turnpiking of roads were, of course, at
work to expand and enrich social and economic life in eighteenth-
century Hertfordshire; but without better roads than ever before
expansion would have been impossible. As for the now well-estab-
lished commercial and professional squirearchy, the concentration
of business and administrative centres on the north bank of the
Thames – which before about 1760 was crossed by only one bridge
– meant that Hertfordshire, within a day's journey of London, was
admirably suited to be the background of their social display, as,
indeed, the high price of houses and estates there testifies. The
county's oldest (at that time almost its only) industry, malting,

throve exceedingly – though, to be sure, its prosperity was due nearly as much to the improved navigation of the rivers Lea and Stort as to the roads. All towns showed a steady expansion as their markets attracted buyers from a wider area and their local products could be distributed further afield. Nor was the countryside without substantial benefit; as early as 1730 it was written that 'the barley of Hertfordshire is so much prized in London that many hundred quarters are sold by that name, of which not one grain was ever sown in this county'. Hertfordshire eggs were famous too and its livestock and farm produce found an eager sale in London markets, the laden southbound wagons returning not only with London-made luxuries but, quite as important, with rags, old straw and night soil to lighten and manure the county's hungry fields. As the century progressed, more and more travel, by coach, horse and foot, infused new life – and perhaps wider ideas of life – into both its inns and its roadside villages. Whenever a Hertfordshire man saw a milestone inscribed 'London ... miles' he had the best of reasons for taking off his hat to it.

The presence of milestones along a road is clear indication of its having been a turnpike road – there are about 100 milestones left in the county, though they tend to disappear when their road is widened. Roughly speaking, all stone milestones belong to the eighteenth century, the iron mileage plates bolted to some ('devised by Mr McAdam', according to one Trust) being added in the early years of the nineteenth. The earliest datable milestones in the county were erected in Barkway and Barley between 1728 and 1732; but a gravestone-shaped one in Hamels Park, Puckeridge (with re-cut lettering), might well be earlier. Most Trusts adopted a standard pattern for the stones along their roads, the chief exception being along A 5 north of St Albans, where each is of different design.

With the rapid development of the iron industry in the Midlands during the latter part of the century, however, came cast-iron milestones. Hertfordshire contains fewer of these than of the stone ones but they are in general easier to see from a passing car. Milestone-spotting, by the way – not always as simple as it appears – can be a pleasant diversion. Sometimes stones are found literally in the middle of a hedge and sometimes on a by-road that was formerly part of a turnpike, while sometimes an old eighteenth-century stone has been moved to a later constructed road. Where stones remain in their original situation it is interesting to note that their placing has on the whole been very accurately surveyed.

So far as I know – though I stand open to correction – only one toll-house survives in the county, and that of a design different from the usual. An ordinary timber-framed cottage with brick in-filling, it stands on the east side of Ayot Green, a little south of Welwyn. Built in 1728, it was taken over by the Welwyn Trust a year or two later and remained in their hands until 1877, when it and another some miles off were together sold for £24 10s. The story goes that in that year, when the toll-bar was removed and the Trust ceased to function, the landlord of the *Red Lion* nearly opposite celebrated the occasion by putting a cask of beer on Ayot Green for all to help themselves.

Now outside the Red Lion also stood a large wooden trough, hand filled, at which horses and cattle could slake their thirst while drivers slaked theirs inside. At just about the time of the cessation of Turnpike Trusts the Metropolitan Drinking Fountain and Cattle Trough Association began to erect by the side of main roads granite troughs with a piped supply, provided with a lower trough for dogs and a push-button fountain for human beings. Only five of these remain in Hertfordshire – at Potters Bar, Hatfield, Bushey, Croxley Green and Rickmansworth – filled for the most part by flowers or rubbish. Nobody seems to take much account of them; but are they not relics, and not insignificant relics, of the horse-drawn age that has gone for ever?

While on the subject of roads may I suggest a few bridges that are worth noting. That over the Ver at St Michael's, St Albans, built in 1765, is the oldest in Hertfordshire, though several others can run it close – the little bridge opposite the disused mill at Tonwell near Hertford, for instance, built in 1798; a bridge at Braughing, carrying B 1368, rebuilt in 1937 but having an old stone plaque in one of its parapets, 'Built in 1769 by William Edwards'; the elegant five-arch bridge over the Colne at London Colney built in 1772, though

6   *A lane at Buckland*

the jettied side rails are post-Second World War. The two arches of the large bridge carrying A 10 over the Rib at Wadesmill and built in 1825 rest on seven central columns, giving the underbelly of the structure an agreeable play of light; its original latticed siderails were replaced only in 1967 as the result of a lorry accident. A fair number of small bridges here and there in the county will, if carefully examined, be found to bear dates in the nineteenth century.

And here, in passing, is another suggestion for roadside-spotting, though applicable only in the south of the county.

From 1667 the City of London was empowered to levy a tax on coal and wine entering from other regions, its yield devoted to rebuilding after the Great Fire a year earlier. Under an Act of 1851 boundary markers were erected alongside waterways, railways and roads at points 25 miles from the General Post Office in St Martin's-le-Grand. Ten years later another Act substituted the then boundary of the Metropolitan Police District, previously erected markers being moved to their new sites. The Coal and Wine Duties were abolished in 1889; but in 1961 the City Corporation repainted all roadside markers and still keeps them in excellent condition.

These roadside markers – 36 in Hertfordshire – are of cast-iron, varying in height between four feet and two feet as the immediately surrounding surface has left them, white painted and bearing both the arms of the City and the citation of the Act under which they were erected or moved; they may be seen from Wormley, through Potters Bar, to Rickmansworth. In addition, two waterside ones – squat stone obelisks from four feet to five feet in height – are alongside the Lea at Wormley and the Grand Union Canal at Rickmansworth respectively. The most conspicuous rail-side marker – a graceful stone obelisk 14 feet high – stands above the main line out of King's Cross between Potters Bar and Brookmans Park stations; Ordnance Survey maps call it the Duty Stone. Fragments of others lie flat at Wormley and Watford. One of rather different design and of cast-iron, not stone, is only a few yards over the county boundary at Northwood, on the main line out of Euston; a similar one can be seen on the St Pancras line near Radlett.

The first railway in Hertfordshire, in 1838, passed through Wat-

7   *Looking north from near Reed*

ford, Berkhamsted and Tring on its way to Birmingham; not for a
good many years, however, did it or its successors in the county
exercise appreciable influence on economic or social life – indeed,
in the 1870s the London and North Western Railway Company was
boosting Watford by offering a free 21-year season ticket to buyers
of houses there of above a certain purchase price, the ticket to go
with the house, not exclusively to the first purchaser. But what the
railways did, of course, was to put Turnpike Trusts into final insolvency. Roads deteriorated once more; even the later Highway
Boards, covering a wider area more efficiently, did little other than
keep them in reasonably usable condition, even though the impact
of London on at least the southern part of the county brought more
and more traffic and the population, from Prime Ministers and
South African diamond magnates to villagers of many generations'
standing, rose steadily. Yet here the general perspective must be
borne carefully in mind – it was not much later that Forster spoke
of the county as 'England meditative'. On the whole it was.

This brief survey, however, has taken us a long distance from
the lanes and by-ways that I was recommending earlier in the chapter. What is there to say about them?

Not much – because, used by the countryman alone, not by the
bona fide traveller, they were the Cinderellas of the roads. Until
relatively recent times all lesser roads were the responsibility of the
various parishes through which they passed, each parish for its
individual section; and since each parish had to foot the bill for upkeep out of its own rates, upkeep consisted almost entirely in dump-
ing a load of stones into the worst potholes and hoping for the best
– except, of course, when a flood or some other climatic vagary
washed the road away altogether, at any rate for the time being.
Thus, for instance, a Hertfordshire farmer-diarist writing of a flood
in the Mimram valley in 1795 (only one of many) speaks of roads
vanishing and bridges washed away, so that 'men that set out on the
Monday morning to work ... could not get home to their families
till the Wednesday or Thursday night following'. Today adequate
drainage and surfacing has enormously reduced such hazards – he
will be an unlucky man indeed who cannot, at the worst, splash

through an occasional puddle.

It remains only to explain my plan for the rest of this book. Other volumes in the series sketch a number of suggested tours through their respective counties, each designed to illustrate one general aspect of them. But Hertfordshire is small – the sixth smallest county in England; the awkward lay-out of its roads has been made plain; and when I came to tracing on the map a series of appropriate tours I found their routes (often by lanes and by-ways) so complicated to describe that little or no space would have been left to deal with what one saw on the way. And then it occurred to me – instead of following a route, why not follow a theme? Why not go in search of churches, country houses, inns or what not, even if only selected examples of each could be given? Why not leave the motorist, cyclist or walker armed with an Ordnance Survey map to choose the route likely to suit him best and to make his own discoveries? After all, it is better that he should see Hertfordshire through his own eyes than through mine.

That, then, is what I have done, though at the same time trying wherever possible to simplify the explorer's task by grouping my theme examples (by no means comprehensive) into convenient areas. The plan necessitates the repetition of certain historical facts, due to their appearing in more than one thematic or topographical context; but the upshot will again be found, I hope, to simplify what might otherwise have meant a tedious search through previous pages.

And one word more. Buildings and landscapes are of immense interest; but both (and a great deal besides) are the works of man. I have done my best to ensure that my buildings are buildings with figures and my landscapes, landscapes with figures, all appearing out of the past to us today. Sometimes at any rate they may be able not only to adorn a tale but also to point a moral.

CHAPTER TWO

Before Hertfordshire
was Hertfordshire

May it not be possible that the man who claims to be at home in every period of the past turns out to be – shall I say, an optimist? I admit freely to being very little at home in what, from its pre-occupation with digging, is often called 'dirt archaeology', though long familiarity with Hertfordshire (plus, of course, the patience of expert friends) has given me a nodding acquaintance with the county's pre-history. Yet while a great deal of exploratory work has been, and continues to be, done both above and below ground in nearly all parts of it, advancing knowledge at a great rate, what chiefly concern us here are established archaeological sites that can be visited – and appreciated – by the non-expert; and to them I venture, though diffidently, to offer myself as guide, with opportunity to expand to some extent the brief sketch of the periods before Hertfordshire was Hertfordshire that I made in my first chapter.

To begin with, however, it will be well to recall the two basic conditions with which early man had to contend in the Hertford-shire we know. The first is geological – chalk hills rimming its northern and western boundaries, with a gentle southward slope, chiefly of clay, towards Middlesex and the Thames valley. Whereas chalk admits of tolerably easy cultivation, clay is more or less unworkable until ploughs of sufficient weight and of adequate design have been evolved to break it up. The second is the density of forest covering virtually the whole region except the hilltops, discouraging penetration and later delaying effective settlement until the laborious process of clearance by primitive tools has made arable fields possible. With these two conditions in mind it is scarcely surprising that down to, and largely including, Roman times habitation was entirely

confined to the uplands or to river valleys. Even the great Roman roads that I mentioned in my first chapter followed the latter – Ermine Street the valleys of the Lea, Rib and Quin, Watling Street the valley of the Ver, Akeman Street those of the Gade and Bulbourne – though certain smaller roads did admittedly penetrate forest areas.

But many centuries before Roman roadmakers got to work the Icknield Way had kept to the Chiltern crest from Royston through Luton to Tring and then into Buckinghamshire. It is probably unnecessary to remind readers that such early 'roads' as this were not constructed things; they were brought into existence by the impact of countless feet, human and animal, without definition, without a settled line of advance, duplicating or triplicating before any obstruction, however temporary, of surface, vegetation or weather – vague trackways up to a quarter of a mile broad. Along the Icknield Way, as I have already said, are the earliest survivals of man in Hertfordshire. On Royston Heath is a Neolithic long barrow or burial mound, 125 feet in length, some 65 feet in width and up to 12 feet in height; excavation about 100 years ago showed that it contained the remains of several people, some inhumed, some cremated, suggesting that they had belonged to different periods. In the immediate neighbourhood are five round barrows, probably rather later in date, varying in diameter from 27 feet to 66 feet and in height from three feet to 12 feet. But round barrows are by no means confined to the Icknield Way – there are at least 30 of them in the county, mostly in or close to river valleys and dating from any period between the early Iron Age and the seventh or eighth centuries of our era. Probably the best known of all, called the Six Hills, lie alongside the Great North Road (B 197) near the south end of Stevenage; they are Roman in origin. In two places, Sandon and Widford, mounds once listed as barrows were in fact – or so it has been suggested – the mounds on which the keeps of medieval castles were built.

Bronze Age finds have been made at various points along the Icknield Way, but except for the barrows near the Royston long barrow no visitable site survives. With the early Iron Age (roughly the fifth century B.C.) our choice begins to increase. The early Iron

9 *Westmill*

Age peoples, driven from their European homes by hordes of Asiatic invaders, brought with them not only, as their name implies, a knowledge of working in iron but also of more advanced constructional techniques – as are shown by three hill forts along the Hertfordshire section of the Icknield Way and elaborate systems of trench fortification almost the full length of Dunstable Downs in Bedfordshire and round Ivinghoe Beacon in Buckinghamshire. These hill forts are at Arbury Banks near Ashwell, Wilbury Hill at Letchworth and Ravensburgh Castle, Hexton. All follow the same pattern – a big enclosure protected by a deep ditch, revetted and further strengthened by a palisaded rampart thrown up by the spoil of the ditch, the entrance to the enclosure being originally flanked by timber-built guard chambers. Inside this enclosure the inhabitants occupied circular huts of wattle and daub, with a strong central wooden pillar and roof of thatch; and inside the enclosure too slept the cattle and other livestock.

Centuries of weather and ploughing have left very little to see at Arbury Banks and Wilbury Hill, though both are worth a visit if it can be paid without inconvenience. Ravensburgh Castle on a hilltop above Hexton is, on the contrary, rewarding – comparable, indeed, with many hill forts in counties famous for such works. Between 400 feet and 500 feet above sea level and oval in shape, it covers a total of 22 acres, its ditch being up to 55 feet in width but by now nearly filled in, its rampart rising to between 16 feet and 18 feet above the enclosure. At its north end the rampart is doubled, one arm of it overlapping the other, as though, it may be, to protect an entrance – the cart track leading up from the village may, in fact, more than suggest its original line of approach, though there is also what appears to be another small entrance at the south-east corner. From every direction the steep slope of the hillside forms a natural glacis and the whole site is one of immense defensive strength; but appreciation of its siting, as well of some of its constructional details, is marred by the trees, first planted about 70 years ago, with which part of it is covered.

To what extent these hill forts served their makers as permanent settlements, transit camps or refuges in times of danger is not clear;

later comers certainly established themselves in some of them, as well as building others of much the same pattern. Those newcomers, so far as Hertfordshire is concerned, were a Belgic tribe known to the Romans as Catuvellauni (what they called themselves we have no idea), migrating from the Champagne region of France, landing in the Thames estuary and advancing north-westwards up the valleys of the Lea and its tributaries. Their arrival is commonly said to date from round about 75 B.C. or rather earlier; before many years they had penetrated as far as the Icknield Way, founding settlements here and there and, aided by a heavier plough with iron instead of wooden coulter, pursuing agriculture on a scale hitherto unknown, yet restless, pugnacious, acquisitive. Though Hertfordshire always remained their heartland, there came a time when, having overrun Bedfordshire, they ruled a great tract of south-eastern England from Essex to Oxfordshire.

Their social structure was military, somewhat resembling in harsher form the feudal system of the Middle Ages. The flower of their tribal army was, however, not the knights but the charioteers, for the Catuvellauni had developed the chariot into a weapon formidable enough to overcome pretty well any opponent. Wood-built and drawn by two horses, each chariot was manned by a driver, a knight and one or more of his followers; it made headlong for the enemy's ranks, discharged its fighting men into his midst, wheeled about and stood a short distance off, ready at a moment's notice either to rescue them in the event of a retreat or to lead a pursuit in the event of victory. Men and horses were trained to superb degree and the feats of which they are known to have been capable are astonishing.

Against such works as hill forts, however, chariot tactics obviously had no place. A new form of defence against the operations of chariot-driving neighbours had to be devised – such long earthworks, sometimes extending for many miles, as can be seen at the north end of St Albans, between A6 and B651 (Beach Bottom) or east of A5 from Mayne's Farm to Gorhambury Drive (Devil's Dyke). Both these are probably surviving lengths of a single earthwork – a ditch of roughly 130 feet wide and up to 30 feet deep, the spoil of the ditch banked up in a rampart on either side and evidently intended to protect the stretch of territory between the Ver and the Lea. And near each end of it is a Belgic fort – the Aubreys at Redbourn and the early tribal capital of the Catuvellauni at Marford, near Wheathampstead.

Because of a hotel at its southern end the Aubreys at Redbourn is not difficult to visit. Covering in all rather more than 22 acres, it consists for the most part of double ramparts up to 14 feet high, the two being separated by a ditch. In parts, however, the outer rampart has been ploughed away and weathering has no doubt reduced the height of both; moreover, the whole site is wooded, making a general view, and thus a clear estimate of its plan, no easy matter. Of the Wheathampstead site, however, a great deal more is to be said.

On the south side of B 653 from Wheathampstead to Lemsford and about a mile from the village of Wheathampstead a side turning called Dyke Lane leads to part of the defences of the Belgic capital – an immense ditch (also, and rather confusingly, known as the Devil's Dyke) 1,400 feet in length, with a greatest width of 130 feet and a greatest depth of 35 feet. A farm track past Beech Dyke Farm, which lies off Dyke Lane, stops short of a return ditch, known as the Slad and parallel to the Devil's Dyke, about 1,200 feet long, 80 feet wide and 25 feet deep. Both are ramparted and both, together with a now lost section near Beech Dyke Farm, formed three sides of the defences of a kidney-shaped enclosure embracing 100 acres, the fourth side no doubt being the, in Belgic times, marshy valley of the Lea. Excavation in 1932 by Sir (then Dr) Mortimer Wheeler brought to light ample evidence of its occupation as an important centre by the early Catuvellauni and the evidence of Caesar in his *De Belle Gallico* makes it a candidate for the scene of his victory over Cassivellaunus, the early Catuvellaunian chieftain.

But before discussing that candidature it may be added that from the Wheathampstead site ran a trackway through Welwyn, where it crossed the Mimram by a ford and where there was a secondary settlement, to Gatesbury Hill near Braughing, where also a settlement stood. Later on, when the Catuvellauni had conquered the tribe, called the Trinovantes, occupying Essex (two of their kings there, by the way, were Cunobelin – Shakespeare's Cymbeline – and Caratacus, or Caractacus, who ended his life a prisoner of Rome) this trackway was extended from Braughing through Bishop's Stortford to Colchester, the seat of Catuvellaunian rule over the region.

It was during Caesar's second reconnaissance raid, in 54 B.C., upon the then unexplored island of Britain – some of his troops are said to have mutinied at being expected to campaign 'outside the limits of the known world' – that he found himself opposed by a confederation of Belgic tribes headed by Cassivellaunus, who carried out a dogged retreat into the very heart of Catuvellaunian territory, their chariots inflicting heavy casualties on even the most disciplined Roman legions until effective retaliation was made by firing not at charioteer or warrior but at the horses. And somewhere in Hertfordshire it was that Cassivellaunus suffered defeat. But exactly where is open to debate – Caesar himself says merely that 'Cassivellaunus' stronghold' was 'of great natural strength and excellently fortified' and 'protected by forests and marshes'. While Wheathampstead would appear the obvious choice from its association with the chieftain, it must be pointed out that nothing whatever of Roman origin has been found either inside the enclosure or in the vicinity – a strange, though perhaps only (from our point of view) unlucky, absence of the inevitable detritus of a hard-fought battle. Further excavation might of course reverse the luck. The older Iron Age hill forts – Arbury Banks. Wilbury Hill, Ravensburgh Castle – can for various reasons be more or less ruled out; but two other possible candidates remain : the Aubreys, with its double rampart but much smaller size, and the strongly entrenched Wallbury Camp at Little Hallingbury, a few hundred yards over the Hertfordshire–Essex border between Bishop's Stortford and Sawbridgeworth.

At any rate, with the defeat of Cassivellaunus resistance to Caesar appears to have ended. Imposing the payment of tribute and claiming hostages, he returned to Gaul. As for the Catuvellauni, after his departure the Wheathampstead settlement gave place to a new one – is it possible to construe this migration as pointing to the scene of their defeat? The new settlement was at Prae Wood (on the road from St Albans to Hemel Hempstead), overlooking the valley of the Ver and nearly opposite the hill on which, in later centuries, St Albans was to stand; it was never heavily defended, nor can it for long have enjoyed the prestige of Wheathampstead, since the transfer of Catuvellaunian rule to Colchester took place within a short time afterwards. But it still remained of some size, with metal-workers, potters and a mint for the striking of coins, at the time of the full-scale invasion of Britain by Aulus Plautius (acting under orders from the Emperor Claudius) in A.D. 43; and the first Roman city of Verulamium sprang up at its edge.

Now in the century between Caesar and Aulus Plautius a change had begun to come over the Catuvellauni. In a word, even so disastrous an event as a defeat by the Romans apparently did not close their eyes to the splendours of Roman civilisation. Gradually – very gradually – pugnacity gave way to trading, to the export of grain, cattle, hides, slaves and hunting dogs and the import of wine, oil, silks and elaborate table ware in pottery, bronze or silver. Quite soon after the establishment of Verulamium they were beginning to rebuild their simple wattle-and-daub huts in larger and more elegant Roman fashion, enjoying a standard of comfort they had never before known – indeed, a fair proportion of Roman villas excavated in the county have turned out to be built over earlier Belgic sites. Once fairly under Roman domination they adopted – with enthusiasm, it would seem – the modes of life, even the modes of culture and thought, of their erstwhile conquerors, becoming finally, if not the sole, at least the principal support of Roman power in the region. Of Roman soldiery there was none hereabouts and it is probable that there were relatively few Roman-born Roman citizens, except those who occupied Government posts or other executive positions; the bulk of the population was composed of Romanised Belgae, whose ancestors of a few generations ago had lived in and through their separate and mutually hostile tribes.

Such, then, were the folk who inhabited both the city of Verulamium and all the outlying settlements in Hertfordshire, pursuing their numerous crafts in conformity with the new styles demanded of them but still in the main following traditional Belgic techniques in agriculture. Let us glance at them, first in Verulamium itself, then elsewhere.

The first Verulamium descended the hillside from Prae Wood to the Ver; it seems to have had very little fortification and, in spite of well laid-out streets, drainage system and other amenities, to have retained to the end an aspect of ready adaptation to rapidly changing circumstances. Nor was the end far off – in A.D. 61 (that is, after only some 20 years) Boudicca or Boadicea, Queen of the East Anglian tribe known as the Iceni, rose in revolt against the Roman conquerors (Roman love of order and good government probably did not make for tactful handling of 'heathen' but proud peoples), sacked Colchester, destroyed Verulamium and descended upon London, where she was captured and slain.

But as the heart of an already important region Verulamium could not afford to remain out of commission. By A.D. 79 it had been rebuilt, this time to larger plan of 200 acres, with Watling Street as its axis but still only lightly defended. In the next century and a half it was to grow into a city of great stature, its flint and brick walls pierced by four great gates, its temples, its public offices, its forum, its theatre and many of its houses – in short all the appurtenances of a great administrative, trading, cultural and social centre – equal in size and dignity to any in the province of Britain. Its citizens could indeed claim to be citizens of no mean city. It had its ups and downs, of course – there was a time in the third century when, due to a change in Imperial policy, it suffered a decline; but that was followed by a marked renaissance of rebuilding and new building even more splendid in scale but less so in architectural style. Then in A.D. 410 came an order – the famous Rescript of Honorius – recalling the legions to a Rome threatened on all sides by the barbarian hordes of eastern Europe; no doubt many Government and provincial officials, as well as patriotic private citizens, went with them, though others remained. Slowly Britain – and with it, of course, Verulamium – left for the first time in 400 years without a strong directing hand, was at the mercy of whatever power-seeking men or peoples chose to take their chance. Long forgotten were the days of Belgic prowess in war; trade was at a standstill; and bit by bit Verulamium fell into decay, while the country as a whole sank into what are usually called the Dark Ages. Vegetation, wild animals and lawless bands took possession of its ruins. Roman bricks from it were used in building the tower of St Albans Abbey. Roman bricks from it appeared in many later houses and churches round about. Even in the eighteenth century, as we learn from a contemporary writer, bricks in cartloads were taken for road-making. Only in the early nineteenth century was archaeological interest aroused in its site, by that time meadow land; tentative excavation continued to whet the appetite for more, what was brought to the surface, though imperfectly understood, plainly hinting at the wealth still to be revealed; but funds were lacking and techniques left much to be desired. In 1930 Mortimer Wheeler and his wife (who died soon afterwards) began the series of scientifically controlled 'digs' that, in justifying all earlier expectations, have converted Verulamium from a purely Hertfordshire into a national possession. In promoting them Lord Verulam, on whose land much of the site stood, and the St Albans Corporation played leading parts; and in 1938 the Corporation established the Verulamium Museum to house and display all principal finds and as a centre of archaeological study. Since 1955 a new series of 'digs' under the supervision of Professor Sheppard Frere employs large numbers of university students of archaeology as well as a pick of voluntary helpers.

Before exploring the hillside upon which much of Verulamium stood it will, I fancy, be profitable to visit the Museum, where an admirable reconstruction of the ancient city in its heyday occupies a prominent position. Only a Roman bird can have seen it so completely yet in such detail, with all its streets and buildings, its walls and, rather surprisingly, the fields inside them. Gates, temples, public buildings, houses and hovels are all reproduced with painstaking accuracy – here, in short, is history come to life. And elsewhere in the Museum too, excellently displayed and described, are innumerable bits and pieces of the frame within which that life was lived – not only its gods and goddesses, the elegance of its larger houses and their fitments, the fine design and craftsmanship of its pottery and metal work, the elaborate prettiness of its coins, but also the daily tools and knicknacks of the people. We catch glimpses of them at work and at play – in their occupations, crafts or agriculture, at the oyster bar, in the forum, at the baths and the theatre, inscribing their letters, gambling, trimming their nails, plucking their eyebrows. And somewhere about the place is the intriguing record of an incident in Roman canine life – a tile which, before firing, received three quick impressions: the paw of a dog, the stone thrown at it and the paw, with claws out, as the startled animal sprang away.

One word of advice I would offer all visitors to the Museum. Before leaving, do not forget to inquire whether any 'digs' are in progress. It is fascinating to watch the meticulous care with which each stratum of pit or trench is ticketed, each spoonful – and I mean spoonful – of earth is examined for what it may contain, the precise position of each find, however trifling, is carefully measured and recorded. What patient devotion goes into such work as this, often carried on in narrowly confined spaces and in cramped postures. And all the time, somewhere behind the scenes, other workers are deftly fitting together hundreds of fragments into their component wholes, docketing, scheduling, plotting, comparing, wringing from them the last shred of evidence they are capable of offering. To watch is surely to receive an admirable lesson in the satisfaction received from work conscientiously carried out. And just to show that the lesson has been absorbed and appreciated, please do not, I suggest, forget to drop a coin or two into the collecting box to be found on the site; something more tangible than devotion is required to bring a 'dig' to a successful ending.

There are still parts of the city, surveyed only by aerial photography, awaiting the excavating gear and scientific method of the experts; many areas already excavated have been filled in again. So that to some extent it is one's imagination that must get to work on the hillside behind the Museum, conjuring in the mind's eye (and with memory of the reconstruction in mind too) the chessboard pattern of streets and all their attendant buildings that lie a few feet below the greensward. But visual aids are not, happily, quite absent. Near King Harry Lane is a stretch of the old brick and flint wall; it is several hundred feet in length, between seven and nine feet wide at the base, rising now to about 12 feet but originally to a height of 23 feet. Outside it is a ditch about 80 feet wide and 20 feet deep; and there are small fragments of wall and ditch elsewhere. Not far away, flint patterning in the grass outlines the guard chambers of the gate through which Watling Street entered the city; there were two arched entrances for traffic and two for pedestrians. A little way along Watling Street inside the walls the footings of a great triumphal arch are still visible. In another part of the site, and well preserved for visitors' inspection, is what has been rather erroneously called the hypocaust; it is, in fact, the large mosaic pavement in a second-century house to the floor of one room of a bath suite of three rooms, all heated (on the Turkish bath principle) to various temperatures by an elaborate system of underground pipes. And so back past the Museum and the forum (the latter about 200 feet by 300 feet, with the basilica, or town hall, on the site of St Michael's church) to the theatre, the only one surviving in Britain.

It was, in fact, the action of a farmer of 1847 in drawing the attention of a local antiquary to bits of unaccountable wall in certain of his fields that first aroused interest in the whole subject of Verulamium. But the excavations made both then and later were all covered in again; not until 1933 was the complete site permanently exposed. There seems, however, little point in dilating upon it here, since an authoritative booklet can be obtained on the spot – indeed, all Verulamium is handsomely, so to speak, documented both here and at the Museum. It will suffice to say that the theatre appears to have been used not only for stage plays and dance festivals but also for bear baiting and cock fighting. It was still in use up to the middle of the fourth century; later it may well have degenerated into a municipal rubbish dump.

Wide, metalled and well cambered roads to ten different destinations, some relatively local, others distant, left Verulamium's four gates; another road hub – or at least an important road crossing – was the Roman town probably called Curcinati. It lay between Puckeridge and Braughing on both sides of B 1368, the now closed Braughing railway station being more or less at its centre. Traditions and stories of its existence had persisted for several centuries, strengthened from time to time by finds of Roman material in its immediate vicinity. A road, its present course little more than a century old, had been driven through it and it had again been pierced by the railway in the 1860s. Yet not until just after the Second World War was serious investigation of the area undertaken and preliminary excavation begun; and then – a piece of atrocious luck – the very experienced amateur archaeologist in charge was compelled by a change of job to leave Hertfordshire. For some years the work remained at a standstill; only in the 1960s has it been to some extent resumed. It follows therefore that whatever estimate of the town's nature and importance it is possible to make must be regarded as, to say the least, tentative. I have an idea that dedicated archaeologists would at present discourage any attempt at all.

It, or part of it, was built on what is now known as Wickham Field, starting roughly from the field's western edge, across railway and road and with the Rib as its eastern boundary; beyond the river lay a Belgic earthwork close to Gatesbury Wood. Its north-south boundaries are so far unknown – to the north it probably did not cross the Rib (which here makes a right-angled bend), since a cemetery (and Roman cemeteries always lay outside the place they served) was found on the edge of Braughing village. At the south end the wall of a Roman building (was it the bath house of the town?) stood close to the river bank half a mile from Braughing station. From air photographs, crop marks, trial excavations and other sources it appears that the town was laid out on the usual Roman grid pattern, with temples, public buildings and so on near its centre; and there are indications that it was walled.

Plainly it can have been nothing like the size of Verulamium; but no other site in Hertfordshire has so far revealed such urban characteristics and the question suggests itself whether it may not have been second in importance only to the great regional capital. Incidentally, one wonders why such a possibility has not led to fuller investigation by some central authority; no doubt the general financial stringency of the times has alone prevented it. Whatever importance the place may have possessed – and it plainly possessed a good deal – fairly certainly derived, in part at least, from its situation at the crossing of two main thoroughfares – Ermine Street and a road from Colchester through Bishop's Stortford to Baldock and eventually to Lincoln. There may in addition have been smaller roads converging on it. That it was at least a big posting station seems a pretty safe assumption, as well a trading centre for what is now East Hertfordshire; it was moreover directly linked by road with Verulamium. Only a great deal of further work will resolve these problems. The visitor today, however, will see nothing but arable fields, woodland, the road, a disused railway cutting, a house or two and the little Rib, all in a pleasantly undulating countryside. Gone are the Romanised Belgae who once inhabited it – or, for that matter, the folk of all the centuries between them and us. It is by the houses they abandoned, the pottery they smashed and threw away, the coins they dropped, the rings and brooches they mislaid and lost that they live on. Most of this Braughing detritus of their civilisation is now in Hertford Museum; here in Wickham Field their ghosts, friendly enough to those who are willing to be friends, keep their own secrets.

And not here alone. In many parts of Hertfordshire the remains of Roman villas and settlements have been discovered, often in the course of road work, pipe-laying, gravel-digging or residential development; almost invariably the exigencies of the moment have led to their destruction after a rapid investigation has been made and their principal relics removed. In some, excavated in more leisurely and thorough fashion between the wars, the claims of agriculture (they stood on agricultural land) have led to the same result. There is no counterpart in Hertfordshire to, say, the Lullingstone villa in Kent, its footings still open to public view; all that the Roman enthusiast can do is to visit certain sites and murmur, 'Here once stood but stands no longer'. At best he may happen upon a 'dig' still in progress – archaeologists are active hereabouts – in which case he will be in his element. But I can make no promises.

One of the most rewarding excavations of recent years has been that of a villa in Gadebridge Park, Hemel Hempstead, by the Ministry of Public Building and Works, which laid bare its history over four centuries of our era. It began in the first as a wooden hut with stone-built bath house alongside. In the second the villa was re-built in stone and the bath house enlarged and equipped with central heating. In the early third century the bath house was again enlarged and two farm buildings, each about 100 feet long, were erected near the villa. These appear to have fallen into disuse later in the century, the period in which, it will be remembered, Verulamium also suffered a temporary decline. Then, with the return of prosperity in the fourth, a two-storey tower like a silo, warmed by hot air under the floors, arose at each end of the villa; a gatehouse was added to the courtyard and servants' quarters were built close by.

At this point – or so it would seem – the owner had a bright idea for adding to his income. Quite near the villa was a spring that may (or so he no doubt claimed) have possessed therapeutic properties; at any rate, he built – or rather, jerry-built – a large bath, 68 feet by 48 feet, evidently for public use. But the many coins found in the spring (probably votive offerings in addition to the entrance fee to the bath) show by their dating that the owner's prosperity from this source was short-lived – a matter of 20 years or so. The bath fell to bits and the owner, a sadder and wiser man, was compelled to wrest a livelihood from his farming alone, building wooden stockades that have the appearance of cattle compounds. In the fourth century it would appear that the main villa was, in part at least, out of use. The servants' quarters were still occupied in the early fifth – and that is the end of the story. Why or how final abandonment of the place occurred cannot be told.

A minor Roman centre in which, at the time of writing, important work is being done is Welwyn. It was here that the Belgic trackway from Wheathampstead to Braughing and beyond forded the Mimram and was made by the Romans into what would now be called a good B road – a section, exposed in the late 1950s by trenching for a water pipe, showed it to have been 30 feet wide, metalled to a depth of three feet, gently cambered and having a ditch on each side. A villa was excavated here in the early years of this century, another in the 1930s, a third is suspected but so far not examined and the recent excavation of wells points to the existence of other dwellings in their immediate neighbourhood. A Romano-Belgic cemetery provided a source of sporadic digging for many years; only its destruction in 1968, when a new road was cut through it, showed by the number of burials that Roman Welwyn must have been a considerably bigger place than had been supposed – and it is certainly true that small fragments of Roman pottery can be dug up in almost any Welwyn garden. A few years ago evidence came to light suggesting that the settlement may possibly have had a mill; and excavation now in progress has unearthed a site that appears to comprise four large buildings in an enclosure nearly 400 feet square, with a canalised river through the middle; in one of those buildings are remains possibly suggesting (I rate it no higher than that) its use for some kind of foundry work. But further investigation will certainly afford scope for speculation over a wide field as new discoveries are made. The site is, however, threatened by a major road change to take place in the early 1970s – just as the cemetery was destroyed by a road a few years ago and the probable site of the Belgic settlement sacrificed to a building estate some years before that. In the past Welwyn has been accepted by archaeologists as a posting station and an agricultural supply point for Verulamium; given a fair chance, how much more may it not turn out to have been?

I mention these two instances at random, as examples of the work done in recent years, or still being carried out, for the most part by amateurs of experience, everywhere in the county – at Rickmansworth, Watford, Sarratt, Aldenham, Bushey, Abbot's Langley, Aldbury, along the Gade valley, Harpenden (where a temple was found), Welwyn Garden City, Hitchin, Baldock and along the Icknield Way, nearly all emphasising the integration of late Belgic into Roman life. My concluding instance shows a young amateur (I wonder what has become of him since) playing an unusual part.

In 1943 a bulldozer at work in a gravel pit at Park Street, a couple of miles south of St Albans, was watched by a refugee German schoolboy. Suddenly the boy gave a shout, frantically signalling the machinist to stop. With a dubious shrug the machinist switched his bulldozer to another part of the pit. Off ran the boy post haste to the Verulamium Museum – would someone please come at once to look at a bit of apparently Roman wall that had just been exposed?

Thus was brought to light a Roman villa with the type of history now familiar to Hertfordshire workers but at that date much less recognised. Originating as a Belgic hut in wattle and daub, with earth floors and storage pits, it was rebuilt in stone during the first century A.D., when it consisted of only three rooms. About a century later several more rooms were added, all joined by an open corridor in rear. In the fourth, after the usual period of decline in the third, it was again rebuilt and a bathroom with hypocaust added; but part of it appears to have been used not as a dwelling house but for agricultural purposes. It was burned down in about A.D. 350 or A.D. 360.

Much evidence of its use and of its occupants was rescued from it; but perhaps the most curious object of all was a Belgic slave chain – uncomfortably short, formidably heavy, with a ring at one end for attachment to a post and at the other a most efficient manacle. In the urgent need for gravel in wartime the whole site, having been (with the forbearance of the contractor) excavated, was again delivered to the bulldozer. And that was that.

CHAPTER THREE

Towns and Villages

It is already agreed, I think, that the majority of readers are motorists – I apologise to the others, adding that I too am of their number. Now is it not a fact that in travelling through a town or village few motorists – especially drivers with their attention on the road ahead – can take in more than the obvious aspects of the place? Admittedly they stop to look at churches or houses or to admire a view. Then they move on. Even when they park the car for a more leisurely exploration, it seldom, I think, occurs to them to look at the place as a whole – to wonder why the church is situated where it is, why the houses are disposed in such and such positions, why a road makes a sudden and apparently meaningless kink. It is an interesting inquiry – really, of course, into surviving evidence of the place's origin and development. Careful observation may sometimes suggest an answer; but may I lay down a few guidelines? Though recent changes will very likely have blurred or, in fact, obliterated much of the past, a map of, say, $2\frac{1}{2}$ inches to the mile may reveal points that the eye does not at first appreciate.

In my first chapter I mentioned Hertfordshire's Saxon settlement pattern of a thousand years ago, today resulting for the most part in a village nucleus surrounded by hamlets or isolated farms often bearing the name of End or Green. An exception to this pattern is the parish of Ardeley, which consists of Ardeley, Cromer, Luffenhall, Moor Green and Wood End, all separate entities and all of roughly equal size. In Ardeley itself are the manor house, or Bury, the church and, close by, the parish pump. The pump is a significant item in the landscape, as very likely showing the whereabouts of the water supply without which no settlement could have estab-

10   Ashwell, church tower and Mill Street

lished itself. The other important settlement factor is, of course, the soil. Ardeley lies in the clay region of Hertfordshire, difficult for primitive ploughs but excellent wheat and barley country. In the chalk region of the heavily wooded west and open downland north early settlers' problems were different but not less vital. And in the Lea valley, for instance, large areas of gravel have proved a bugbear to farmers from time immemorial.

It may be, by the way, that another un-nucleated village is Hertingfordbury, lying on gravelly soil above the Mimram with one settlement (a good deal enlarged in the course of last century) running down the hillside towards the river and other ones at Birch Green, Cole Green, East End Green, Letty Green and Staines Green. And I should like to know more about the Mundens, Great and Little. Though they comprised two separate manors at the time of Domesday Book and were always separate parishes, do they in fact represent an early un-nucleated settlement over a rather large area, whose component parts are Dane End, Green End, Haultwick (locally pronounced Aartick), Nasty, Potters Green and Levens Green? But in neither of these cases should I wish to appear dogmatic.

Poor soil may very well account, in part at least, for the disappearance during the Middle Ages of a dozen or more Hertfordshire villages, many of them lying on sticky, intractable boulder clay, the detritus of Ice Age glaciers. Some are no more than names in documents, their whereabouts unknown; of a few traces can still be seen on the ground – at Chesfield near Graveley, Wakeley between Cottered and Westmill, Caldecote near Ashwell, for instance. All these sites, as well as others where village traces have vanished, are now represented by single farms. In counties where building was normally in stone excavation sometimes reveals the foundations of medieval village houses; Hertfordshire's abundance of timber for house building has unfortunately denied that evidence. All that one can hope to find are the squarish, beaten-earth platforms on which the wooden houses stood and the sunken village street between them; in summer grass or crops may make even these discoveries precarious. At Chesfield there are the ruins of a

11 *St Albans, Fishpool Street*

thirteenth-century church and at Caldecote the fourteenth-century church is still in use. The brief history of these deserted villages is always difficult to trace; but a popular belief that they were wiped out by the Black Death of 1348 and 1349 is inadequate as against poverty or exhaustion of the local soil and the lure of better living in places nearer to a highway. Pendley, near Tring, was deliberately destroyed by a fifteenth-century lord of the manor in the creation of a park.

Throcking lies on a hilltop; in the valley to the east of it, between a loop in the road and the long hedge of a ploughed field, can be seen what would appear to be faint traces of an earlier Throcking – though, since no proper investigation has so far been made, I mention it only tentatively. Yet it leads me to another point – that in the course of their history quite a number of villages have moved from their original sites (usually near the church), always to a highway, where trade was to be picked up. Among them are Codicote, Thundridge, Redbourn, King's Langley and St Paul's Walden. Stevenage (impossible in these days to think of it as the village it once was) originated in Saxon days where the church and manor house were later built. Much the same happened at Buntingford. Sarratt is a more puzzling case. As late as the closing years of the seventeenth century it apparently clustered round the church; nowadays church and manor house stand isolated a mile away from the large Green (with pump in the middle) fringed by houses dating in some cases from the seventeenth and eighteenth centuries. What is the reason for so late a migration?

But Hertfordshire's best example of a moved site is St Albans. Before the Romans came the principal Belgic regional centre was, as we already know, first at Wheathampstead, then the hilltop of Prae Wood, overlooking the Ver valley and at that epoch heavily forested. The Romans, when they established themselves in Britain after A.D. 43, built the first Verulamium down the hillside from Prae Wood – Bluehouse Hill it is called today – to the Ver, where it protected a ford; but it was destroyed in A.D. 61 by Boudicca. Whereupon there grew up a second Verulamium, this time along Watling Street – a Verulamium that endured for 300 years or more though in its last stages, in the words of Sir Mortimer Wheeler, 'a nucleated slum'.

At a date traditionally said to be A.D. 303 but, as has lately been argued, possibly a century earlier, the martyrdom of St Alban may have been followed by the erection of a shrine on the hilltop where he suffered death. If so, it gave way to a church and monastery – the Abbey – built and endowed with large estates by the Saxon king, Offa of Mercia, in 793 beyond the east end of the royal town of Kingsbury, where St Michael's bridge and Kingsbury mill now are and on the opposite side of the Ver from Verulamium. By the tenth century the Abbey was already attracting so many pilgrims, for whom accommodation was found in the little township clustering round its gates, that Abbot Wulsin diverted Watling Street from the middle of the now ruined Verulamium, up Holywell Hill, past the Abbey, down George Street and Fishpool Street, and over the Ver to rejoin its old route. At one end of this diversion he built St Stephen's church and at the other St Michael's; the third of his churches, St Peter's, marks the northern limit of the suburb created by him beyond his market place, which stretched from High Street to St Peter's Street and from Chequer Street to French Row. In due course also the royal town of Kingsbury was sold into Abbey possession and its ramparts destroyed – the bend in the middle of Fishpool Street and the houses standing on an embankment well above road level show where part of those ramparts ran.

Thus by the time of the Norman Conquest St Albans, or rather, the centre of it, had assumed much of the shape we see today. Later the entrance to the town from London was again diverted from St Stephen's to Sopwell Lane. Medieval prosperity and dictatorial control by the Abbots led to some, though not much, expansion from its early huddle round the Abbey; but at the same time that huddle was increased (as happened almost everywhere else) by encroachment on the open spaces of the market, which soon became cut up into narrow streets and alleys between blocks of building – in fact, the present plan behind the Town Hall.

Then followed a long period in which, bit by bit, houses appeared along roads formerly free of them – along Hatfield Road (formerly

Cock Lane), for instance; but no general expansion occurred until the turn of the eighteenth and nineteenth centuries. Then a new entry into the town – London Road – took the place of the narrow Sopwell Lane in 1794, Victoria Street was constructed in 1824 from an old and winding lane towards Hatfield, and in 1833 Verulam Road replaced George Street and Fishpool Street as the town's main exit to the north-west. Harpenden Road, though it had been turnpiked as early as 1727, showed little sign of development. As the century progressed both new roads and new estates appeared, especially between the town centre and the railway station, which was opened in 1868, and also along the new London Road. Between the two World Wars both housing estates and industrial works established themselves in increasing numbers round the perimeter and the last quarter of a century has seen an even more rapid residential expansion.

It will be noticed that St Albans (except for a wall surrounding the conventual buildings of the Abbey) was never a walled town – nor was any other in Hertfordshire, even though Hertford itself grew up round two *burhs*, or fortified townships, built by Edward the Elder in 912 and 913 to counter Danish raids across the Lea, at that time the boundary between Saxon England and the Danelaw. He also charged the surrounding region with their upkeep, thus inaugurating what soon became the Shire (Anglo-Saxon, *scir*, an area of local administration) of Hertford. One *burh* stood on each bank of the river, surrounded by a wooded stockade. That on the north side, however, with its market place at Old Cross, enjoyed only a very short life; by 1086, the date of Domesday Book, Hertford had become a single *burh*, or borough, situated on both banks. But before that the southern (and surviving) *burh* also had its market place – and a church too, St Nicholas, just as the northern one was served by St Mary the Less – both churches were long ago demolished. Hertford is therefore, in its essential structure, a double town with two market places.

But strategically well sited though it may have been in Edward the Elder's day, economically it was much less so. Briefly, it lay on no big thoroughfare to London or anywhere else – Ermine Street, the

Roman road from London to York, ran several miles to the east, crossing the Lea at Ware. And the Lea itself, dubiously navigable for many centuries, was inevitably controlled by the men of Ware, who lived lower down its course and were determined to frustrate Hertford's nascent malting industry. All through the Middle Ages and later Hertford and Ware were at loggerheads over the control of the river – a rivalry not even today without faint echoes in the secret estimation of each town for the other.

From the castle on the south bank a road, the present Fore Street, was soon built to connect the borough with Ermine Street near Ware; later a road branched from it near the borough boundary, crossing Hertford Heath and joining Ermine Street at Hoddesdon. Then houses began to appear along Cowbridge and St Andrews Street, both of which were well populated in the fourteenth century, and later along West Street, still a picturesque by-road. In spite of the severe handicaps of unfortunate siting and the opposition of Ware, the borough did slowly develop, dependant to a certain extent, perhaps, on the castle – some pargetted houses close to Parliament Square were built as Government offices when Elizabeth I took refuge there from plague in London. Whether the medieval priory of St John, now demolished, exercised any influence is doubtful. Otherwise, and apart from its malting, the borough had little more than a regional market for its support, the market place extending from the present Shire Hall back to the river at the end of Bull Plain at Folly Bridge – Hertford's oldest surviving inn, the *Salisbury Arms* (formerly the *Bell*), which was a going concern in 1431, stands on the edge of it. As at St Albans, however, encroachment steadily reduced its physical size, though the market continued vigorously until less than a century ago to spread over as much of it as remained – that is, over Salisbury Square and Bull Plain – intersected by Maidenhead Street and Railway Street, both roughly parallel to Fore Street and most likely of about the same age. It may be that the narrow alley called Honey Lane, turning out of Maidenhead Street, was where medieval honey was sold, though the name was bestowed in other places upon any muddy way; and Bircherly Green, formerly Butchery Green and now a bus station and car park, may have been where the butchers congregated just outside the market area.

When the castle passed out of royal hands Hertford's importance rested, apart from its market and a certain amount of malting and brewing, entirely on its status as county town and seat of Quarter Sessions in a period when the Justices had entire control of county government. But that did little for its economic development, which languished with every passing year. Only since the arrival of the railway in 1843, and more recently of motor traction, has the place substantially expanded, though its malting industry is dead.

Elsewhere too in Hertfordshire village development has been influenced by castles – at Anstey, Benington and Pirton. Before its migration to Watling Street, Redbourn lay round the Norman church at Church End; close by is the Iron Age hill fort, also used by the Romans, the Aubreys. It is tempting to believe that this proximity may not be purely accidental. Bygrave, Essendon, Welwyn and Hatfield probably developed not round a castle but round a manor house and the church first established by the lord of the manor. At Bygrave the moated site of the manor house may still be seen; Hatfield speaks for itself.

It was naturally, however, along ancient roads or at road junctions that the majority of Hertfordshire towns grew up – Cheshunt and Ware along Ermine Street; Royston at the intersection of Ermine Street and the Icknield Way; Baldock at the intersection of the Icknield Way and a Roman road from Bishop's Stortford to Biggleswade in Bedfordshire; Bishop's Stortford at the intersection of the same road, which continued into Essex, and another (running along South Street and out by Northgate Street) from London to Cambridge; Watford and Berkhamsted along the Roman Akeman Street. At Cheshunt, Ware, Baldock and Bishop's Stortford there is evidence of Roman occupation; the others are post-Roman in date. The Norman castles at Bishop's Stortford and Berkhamsted (there was a pre-Conquest market at Northchurch) were both built after settlement had been effected close by, serving to confirm and enlarge it. Watford appears in Domesday Book only as the manor of Cashio, with a minute population; not until nearly 100 years later does it emerge as a township. Hoddesdon, until the eighteenth century 'a hamlet in the parish of Broxbourne', developed during the Middle Ages at the fork of Ermine Street and a lesser road to Stanstead Abbots. Buntingford had begun to descend from its hilltop at Layston, where the ruined church of St Bartholomew is, by the mid-thirteenth century, when the predecessor of St Peter's was first built alongside the high road; and among smaller villages at road junctions may be included Cottered and Watton. The first had until 1969, the second still has, a pump at the junction.

Bishop's Stortford and, a few miles to the south, Sawbridgeworth, are worth a moment's attention for curious bulges in the county boundary that occur on their east sides – bulges that are, in effect, bridgeheads to protect fords over the Stort and the markets that early developed in both places; it seems likely that the castle at Bishop's Stortford, built by the Bishop of London, was sited alongside the river rather than on the adjacent Windhill to give the ford further protection. The Bishop's Stortford market, by the way, originally occupied the road crossing now rendered difficult for traffic by the Corn Exchange and close to the *George Hotel*, which is of medieval foundation; that at Sawbridgeworth can be traced by its perimeter streets – Bell Street, Knight Street, Station Road and London Road. But of all roadside towns in Hertfordshire the most interesting is Ware.

In *The Brewing Industry in England 1700-1830* Peter Mathias calls the Lea Valley 'the cradle of the malting industry in Britain'. Ermine Street gave access to the abundant barley country of east and north Hertfordshire and the counties of north Essex, Cambridge and Huntingdon – even of Suffolk and the western part of Norfolk. At the intersection of road and river, Ware could scarcely help becoming from at least the early Middle Ages the foremost malting town in the kingdom – indeed, until only the last few years it abounded in malthouses big and small. So consistently great was its barley intake that as early as 1663 a long stretch of Ermine Street was, as I said in my first chapter, placed under the control of the county Justices of Hertford, Cambridge and Huntingdon – England's first turnpike road – to prevent its destruction by loaded wagons and pack horses; malt could be sent to London, its principal destination, either by road or, as navigation improved, by the Lea. But this centuries-old industrial activity was imposed upon a town basically medieval in structure – a High Street containing a huge triangular market place with the church at its apex and, back from the houses on the south side of the street, innumerable narrow strips of land, now largely covered by small buildings and sheds, down to the river bank with its gazebos (nearly all demolished, alas) overlooking the stream. Even if there may be some difficulty in discerning the full layout on the ground a medium-scale map will make it plain. Gradual encroachment on the market place produced Kibes Lane, East Street, West Street and the various blocks of building between them and the High Street – a scene that in its totality Professor W. G. Hoskins urges 'should be preserved as one of the historic town centres of England'. Later development created Musley Lane, Collet Road and the Bourne as a kind of bypass; but that and High Street put together are now inadequate to modern traffic and drastic change is planned for the immediate future. Change is no doubt inevitable; what is not is that little by little all High Street and the area down to the river are being dissolved by what Hoskins calls 'the acid of modern development'. At Ware there is little merciful dilution of the acid by those who could and should have diluted it.

Two other towns at road crossings may profitably be looked at. Northbound travellers along the Great North Road – that is, if they do not prefer A 1(M) – meet at Baldock an irritating check at the bottom of the wide market place in High Street, where they must turn right into White Horse Street and, after a few hundred yards, left again to resume their northward course. White Horse Street is, in fact, a diversion of the ancient Icknield Way, with the traffic lights at its crossing of the Roman road, now called Clothall Road, from Bishop's Stortford, on the east side of which a Roman settlement was excavated almost 40 years ago. The present town of Baldock was founded by the Knights Templar in the twelfth century, though a belief, fostered by the pundits over many years, that its name derives from Baghdad is not unassailable; in building it the Templars diverted both the Icknield Way and the Roman road in the creation of a town centre with market place and church – and also, be it noted, of a direct route to London.

Further east along the Icknield Way, Royston, at its crossing with Ermine Street, has so far revealed no Roman remains, though a settlement of some kind might be inferred from its situation. The first known of the town is the establishment in the late twelfth century of an Augustinian priory and the grant of a market and fair in 1189. Two more fairs came into existence in the next 50 years. All these were originally held in a cigar-shaped open space at the road crossing, now largely taken up by High Street, King Street and Lower King Street – the block of millstone grit, popularly known as Rohesia's Cross, is probably the socket of an old market cross. Only a tiny open space north of the cross now survives. The present market place, east of Ermine Street, came into use in the eighteenth century: a book of 1745 says of this market that 'it is almost incredible what a multitude of Corn Merchants, Maltsters and other Dealers in Grain do constantly resort to it, and what a vast Number of Horses Laden with Corn do on the Market Days fill all the Roads round it'. Royston's heyday came, however, with the coaching era, when it expanded appreciably; but its position on only a branch railway line, opened in 1850, and the collapse of the market, brought about a steady decline to a town of very secondary importance.

The extent to which Royston's fortunes have been influenced by its difficult administrative set-up would be interesting to speculate upon. At its first establishment it lay at the junction of five parishes – Barkway, Reed and Therfield in Hertfordshire, Melbourn and Kneesworth in Cambridgeshire. In 1540, when the priory was suppressed, an Act made it a united ecclesiastical parish and two and a half centuries later a united parish Vestry, though for wider purposes its division between the two counties was maintained. The Local Government Act of 1894 continued to split it administratively into two; only three years later was it incorporated wholly into Hertfordshire.

What has gone before will have made abundantly plain the part played by a successful market in the expansion of an early settlement into a thriving town. But not all markets were successful. In the late thirteenth century Standon, lying a mile or so east of Ermine Street, became a borough and established a market; a couple of centuries later both borough and market lapsed, the wide main street of that attractive village being the only relic of the latter. Similarly, at Codicote the open space opposite the *George and Dragon*, approached by roads from several directions, is the scene of a thriving medieval market that vanished in mid-sixteenth century. Again, what happened to the market at Ashwell, (a borough at the time of Domesday Book), sited between church and village street and with a later-fifteenth-century market house, now the museum, overlooking it? The size of the fourteenth-century church suggests prosperity even in the decades following the Black Death; but neither of the early county historians – Sir Henry Chauncy in 1700 or Nathaniel Salmon in 1728 – mentions the holding of a market in his day.

Several Hertfordshire towns that I have not so far included in this brief survey cluster round their old markets – Hemel Hempstead between church and High Street and Tring between church and Akeman Street are two of them. Watford still has its spine, so to speak, in the narrow High Street that winds laboriously up from the river Colne to the market place beyond the church, the northern limit of which is marked (with pretty certainly unwitting historical fitness) by the recently blocked roadway near the *Joseph Benskin* inn – originally a large rectangular open space containing (until it was burned down in the 1850s) the half-timbered market house. Off both sides of High Street ran several score of huddled, insanitary alleys and closes, the last of which were demolished only during the 1920s in the building of a covered retail market that finally freed the High Street of its centuries-old weekly clutter. A market had first been granted to the little settlement in the early twelfth century; by 1290 it ranked as a borough, though it does not appear later to have held borough status; even in the early nineteenth century it had stocks and pound, its communal pump and its night watchmen, while the majority of people were occupied in agriculture. Though transformation from market town to industrial centre occupied a good deal of the latter part of that century, it was only in the third decade of this one that the sale of corn, foodstuffs, horses and much besides ceased where cars, motor-bikes, buses and lorries now create an atmosphere far less salubrious.

A change of market site has also taken place at Hitchin – to a cleared space east of the church from the old one in the middle of the town. Approached from Sun Street, Bucklersbury, High Street and various narrow passage-ways, the old market place originally extended from the bottom of Tilehouse Street to the south end of Bancroft, where it abutted on the churchyard. Throughout the Middle Ages it was the centre of Hertfordshire wool-dealing. But by 1470 there is evidence of encroachment – first by market stalls that were no longer removable, then by timber-built houses developed from the permanent stalls. A century later it had been reduced to a fraction of its old size and one or two buildings that still face it might well belong basically to the early seventeenth century. At its south east corner stood the *Angel* inn, a going concern in 1450, continuing in licence until 1956 but now demolished. As token of its long continued importance in the town, a new Corn Exchange was built to dominate it in 1853. But even then increasing traffic had begun to interfere with its smooth transaction of business; yet it did not finally go out of use until about 1930, when a slum area beyond the river Hiz was demolished to provide its present site.

At the south end of the original market place a Carmelite priory was founded in 1317 and, not far away, the Biggin, a Gilbertine nunnery, in 1362. Before long we hear of the streets now called Bridge Street and Queen Street – the latter once called Dead Street, from a tradition that every one of its inhabitants died in a seventeenth-century outbreak of plague. Tilehouse Street, still Hitchin's most picturesque quarter, bore that name in 1460, and so did Bucklersbury, the street of the armourers – and at the same date Bancroft was Bancroft, derived no doubt from 'bean croft', with its northern end known as Silver Street in 1556. Near its junction with what is now High Street was Portmill Lane, so called also in 1556, where beside the Hiz stood the town mill. Then for several centuries the place seems to have undergone little expansion. The area between the rear of Bancroft and Bedford Road is still largely open space – where in earlier days the town archery butts were situated and later cricket was played. But with the coming of the railway in 1850 the whole region between town centre and the station was quickly built over. Nowadays a much bigger and still rising population has brought into the built-up area such formerly outlying points as Bearton Green, Highover, Oughton Head and Walsworth, though Charlton (birthplace of Sir Henry Bessemer), separated from the town by the park of Hitchin Priory, still, for the time being at least, retains much of its rural charm.

Finally there are places grouped not round a market but round a green. The most conspicuous of them are Broxbourne and Harpenden, each with green and church adjoining and each close to a thoroughfare, though the Luton–St Albans road at Harpenden can claim no history to compare with Ermine Street at Broxbourne – so that while Broxbourne, as one would expect, was always of some importance Harpenden remained an inconspicuous, albeit pretty, village until a century or less ago. In 1868 the Midland Railway brought its main line through Harpenden and eleven years later a branch line was opened at Hemel Hempstead. At that time the village's sole claim to attention was its annual race meeting on the Common, which, in the words of the county historian, John Edwin Cussans, writing in the 1870s, made 'travelling in a first class carriage of the Midland Railway a danger to men and an impossibility to ladies', while a guide book of 1903 warns prospective visitors 'not to choose the day of the annual races' Yet for the rest of the year the Common was extremely attractive; the village lay convenient to the business executives of Luton, St Albans and even London; the motor-car came to compete with the railway service; and in 1953 Sir Nikolaus Pevsner could speak of the 'hundreds of phony half-timbered residences of well-to-do Londoners which have grown up in the last 30 years'. It is now an urban district with a population that would have left its people of a century ago gasping; yet in spite of so drastic a change in its fortunes it retains plain evidence in Church Green of its beginning in Saxon days.

Among other 'green' villages may be included Westmill, Newnham, Braughing, and Preston, each with a pump at its centre

14 *South front, Hatfield House*

Northaw in the south, Abbot's Langley and Aldbury in the west, in the middle Weston and in the north Therfield and Sandon are all rewarding to visit.

There is, however, one Hertfordshire village that falls into none of the categories I have mentioned. It is Reed, about three miles south of Royston, a short mile east of Ermine Street and on the crest of the Chilterns, with magnificent views northwards over Bedfordshire and Cambridgeshire along the crest road from Ermine Street to Barkway. Apart from its curiously scattered layout the casual visitor will at first see nothing to arouse his curiosity; but examination of a map shows that the gentle slope southward from the crest road – the slope on which the village stands – is divided into a number of squares intersecting or isolated. A closer look at the ground confirms what the map has shown – sometimes a lane, sometimes a ditch forms a boundary line of these various squares, at times plainly to be traced, at others lost.

There are interesting facts to note about the history of Reed. Saxon work can be seen in the church – one possible explanation of the Saxon origin of Reed's name is 'enclosure', though other authorities derive it from 'rough ground'. Domesday Book suggests an area of about 1440 acres and a population of about 200 – a considerable population for so small a place; both area and population have not appreciably changed from that day to this. Dotted about the southern slope are eight medieval homestead moats, or the remains of them, earthwork protections for houses against marauders human or animal. But the medieval common fields, in which nearly every villager held land in narrow strips, are thrust away on to the northern and less sunny slope. A map of 1808 marks – again on the southern slope – a number of what it calls 'ancient enclosures'.

Fairly plainly, this southern slope, watered by a few springs from the underlying chalk, has from Saxon times been sought after and guarded, though its soil is no better than that of the neighbouring countryside. But that does not explain the meaning of the squares.

Both Ermine Street and the crest road are Roman. Many years ago there were excavated near the village a number of statuettes of

Roman deities and of silver plates bearing their images, as though a shrine had once existed there. These and other discoveries as well point to Roman occupation of the site; and the suggestion has been put forward that Reed was in its beginning an area parcelled out in the square allotments, so to speak, granted to Roman soldiers when they were demobilised – small holdings, rather, where they could settle and make a livelihood. In two places in England and many in Europe this process of centuriation, as it is called, has been observed and its nature proved. It is unfortunate that the field worker who might have solved the riddle of Reed died a few years ago after having made preliminary investigation into maps, documents and surface inspection of the site but before he could begin the only investigation likely to yield decisive results – excavation at key points to discover what Roman material beneath the soil might throw light on the original nature of the place.

Reed must, alas, remain an enigma – for the present at least.

CHAPTER FOUR

Castles and
the Like

If the word 'castle' brings to mind romantic ruins in equally romantic surroundings, be prepared for a measure of disappointment; only one Hertfordshire castle achieves, and one approaches, such a conception. But there are others, far less striking no doubt, though certainly of no less interest – as examples of the prototypes from which all more imposing strongholds were later to spring. It is as such – even if a first glance causes bewilderment – that they deserve a visit, whether or not the visitor professes to be a military historian.

On the whole, Hertfordshire has been a peaceful county – at any rate since the Middle Ages, when peace was everywhere and all the time as brittle as an eggshell. Its best known involvement in hostilities (that is, since Caesar's affair at Wheathampstead) came during the Wars of the Roses, when two battles were fought at St Albans and one in the area between Barnet and South Mimms.

The first St Albans battle, in 1455, when Yorkist forces broke into the middle of the Lancastrian-held town from the south, ended in the capture of Henry VI, who was taken next day to London – a tablet on a wall at the corner of Victoria Street marks the spot at which the Duke of Somerset, Henry's most powerful supporter, was slain 'underneath an alehouse' paltry sign, *The Castle* in St Albans'. The second battle, in 1461, reversed the earlier Lancastrian defeat by releasing the king; after a vain attempt to advance up Fishpool Street, a rapid switch brought the Lancastrian forces to the northern outskirts of the place, cutting the Yorkists in half and defeating one half on Barnard's Heath (on A 6), the other in the town itself. That night the Lancastrian soldiery butchered and looted to their hearts' content – it is said that when Queen Margaret, who had come to rejoin her husband, left the town the Abbey's most costly jewel left with her.

Ten years later the battle of Barnet was fought on Gladsmuir Heath, where the stone obelisk, erected in 1740 alongside A 1000 beyond Hadley Common, marks its approximate site; there Warwick the Kingmaker was slain and the whole Lancastrian cause defeated. Contested in a heavy mist, the turning point of the battle came when a contingent of Lancastrians, returning from the pursuit of the defeated Yorkist right wing, were mistaken for the enemy and decimated by their own friends – a misadventure which a few readers may find not wholly inconceivable from their personal war-time knowledge.

None of these battles centred round a castle; nevertheless there had been castles in Hertfordshire long before the Wars of the Roses – indeed, the increasing use of gunpowder during the fifteenth century was quickly rendering obsolete the few that still survived in opera-tional condition at that period. Not counting Iron Age and later earthworks and with just possible exceptions of Hertford and Bishop's Stortford, all Hertfordshire castles were first built by the Normans – certainly the exceptions (if indeed they were exceptions) were rebuilt by them, since they conform, as do the others, to the invariable Norman plan of raising a mound, or motte, surmounted by, at first, a wooden keep and surrounded by a ditched and palisaded area, the bailey, where the garrison lived. Later, of course, as can be seen at Berkhamsted, Bishop's Stortford and to a lesser extent Benington, timber gave place to masonry; the rest of the castle sites in Hertfordshire are now no more than the motte and a series of ditches. Whether some of them ever saw masonry is a moot point.

Berkhamsted, the survivor nearest to its complete state, is well known to the traveller on the main line out of Euston; from the train the curtain wall and inner moat, the motte with its ruined keep and the well-tended lawns that overlie the foundations of many castle buildings – lawns which sheltered well-known London statues during the Second World War – are plainly visible. In 1838, how-ever, it was the railway that sliced through and demolished a large section of the southern outer defences, including the main gateway

16   The Main Hall, Moor Park, Rickmansworth

and barbican, in building Berkhamsted's first station at the end of Castle Street – salutary reminder that vandalism is not confined to the present day, though it must be admitted that in 1838, and for long afterwards, the castle precincts were more esteemed by courting couples, its ruins by children in search of a playground and its ditches in winter by skaters, than as an important relic of Berkhamsted history. In later years the reconstruction of a road on the west side did further damage to the outer defences; but the guardianship of the whole site since 1930 by the Ministry of Public Building and Works is guarantee against even the most determined modern vandal.

Here it was that William of Normandy, near the completion of an encircling movement round London, received the submission of the Saxon nobles and 'promised that he would be a kind lord to them' – a promise of no greater value than that made by any other ruthlessly power-seeking man. That there was a defensive work at Berkhamsted when he did so is doubtful, though the site might appear favourable to one; it was his half-brother, Robert, Count of Mortain, to whom this manor (among many others) was granted, who first threw up a motte and dug a ditch round it, fortifying both with timber. But only a century later, when Robert's stronghold had been destroyed, was it rebuilt with stone keep and curtain walls – by Thomas Becket, who held it as Henry II's Chancellor. Further strengthening of the position took place in succeeding years; and then, in 1216, it was besieged by Louis, Dauphin of France, in his aid to the Barons (and through them, he hoped, to himself) against King John.

Commanding the defenders on the King's behalf was a German, leader in many sallies (one of them disarming a party of Barons as they sat comfortably at table) and a determined soldier; but the besiegers battered the walls with huge stones hurled from catapults called mangonels to such effect that at the end of a fortnight capitulation had become inevitable. Until 1254 the castle remained in its war-damaged condition; then the walls were put once again in good order and a great three-storeyed tower roofed with lead was built as a keep on the motte, as well as dwelling houses in the various

7   *Ashridge, the chapel*

bailies – a document of half a century later speaks of the King and Queen's Chamber, the Queen's Chapel, the Nurse's Chamber and so on.

In 1361 it housed King John of France, captured at Poitiers, whom we shall meet again at Hertford; a little later it was in the hands (until he lost both it and his head) of Piers Gaveston, favourite of Edward II, with whom he is traditionally said to have played pitch-and-toss on Berkhamsted Common. But its best-known holder was Edward III's son, the Black Prince – his favourite residence in England and scene of his honeymoon with his cousin Joan, the Fair Maid of Kent, when he entertained the whole Royal family for five days. It was from here in 1376 that he set out for the last time, to end his stormy life at Westminster only a few days afterwards.

Another famous name connected with the castle is that of Geoffrey Chaucer, who was Clerk of Works in the early fifteenth century, though it is doubtful whether he ever visited it. The last resident of consequence was Cicely, Duchess of York, who died here in 1495; thereafter it was left unoccupied, to be described in the sixteenth century as 'much in ruin'. Its stones were taken in Elizabethan times to build Berkhamsted Place (demolished in 1968) on the neighbouring hilltop; in the very early nineteenth century the inner bailey was an orchard, the outer a farm.

In the last chapter I outlined the structural development of Hertford from the time when Edward the Elder established two *burhs* near the confluence of the rivers Lea, Mimram and Beane in the early tenth century. Their defences can have been no more than palisades sheltering the entire population. For them William of Normandy substituted on the south bank a motte-and-bailey castle, one of a ring of such castles surrounding London – the motte, now no more than a shabby pimple barely 20 feet high, can be seen near the entrance to the Castle grounds from the Wash. This entrance, by the way, flanked by stone towers, is on the site of the old guardhouse; between it and the Wash formerly stood drawbridges over the inner and outer moats, the barbican and an outer guard-house.

Within and to the left of this modern entrance there grew up

in succeeding centuries all the principal buildings of a royal castle
and residence, running for 200 or more feet parallel to the twelfth-
century masonry wall surrounding the inner bailey. At their south
end the wall turned westwards to a still surviving postern gate and
tower, once fronted by a drawbridge over the inner moat and, beyond it, a guardhouse on the outer moat – both these last have long
since vanished; indeed, all the outer defences of the castle are now
either built over or levelled. Turning northwards at the postern
gate, the wall was next pierced by a big fifteenth-century gatehouse,
also fronted by a drawbridge, from which it returned along the bank
of the Lea to the Keep on its motte.

All the castle's principal buildings, including the Keep, had, however, disappeared by the mid-eighteenth century, though it was said
in 1876 that the base of a small portion then survived. Apart from
stretches of the curtain wall, only the western gatehouse – and
that virtually rebuilt in Gothic style at the turn of the eighteenth
and nineteenth centuries – remains; this it is that is today known
as the Castle. At the same period the inner moat was filled in, to
create the lawns that have provided so pleasant a setting to two
centuries of history. But long before that the Castle had ceased to be
Crown property; in 1628 Charles I granted it to William Cecil,
second Earl of Salisbury, and in Salisbury hands it has been ever
since – in 1911 the then Marquess leased it to the town at a pepper-
corn rent as municipal offices and public park. It is worth noting, by
the way, that among its vanished buildings was one housing a school,
kept in the early eighteenth century by a certain John Worsley,
two pupils of which were the firebrand politician, John Wilkes, and
the philanthropist, John Howard.

Between William of Normandy and Elizabeth I nearly every
sovereign resided at Hertford at one time or another during his
reign – considerations of State apart, it lay at a convenient distance
from London and in the midst of good hawking and hunting country.
But in the Middle Ages, before the royal supremacy had been
established beyond conflict, its many Governors, though holding a
royal appointment, sided sometimes with the King, sometimes with
the Barons still struggling to maintain their own petty sovereignties.

Fortunately in 1216 Walter de Godarville was a King's man; for in that year Louis, Dauphin of France, on his way to Berkhamsted, besieged it for three weeks – and captured it, though Walter appears to have been well treated by him. In the next year, however, Louis was defeated at Lincoln and made the best of his way back to France, disappointed of his hope of eventually securing the English throne.

A prisoner here for 11 years was David Bruce II, King of Scotland (son of Robert Bruce), captured at the battle of Neville's Cross in 1346. With him came his Queen, Joan, daughter of Edward II, to whom separate living accommodation in the castle buildings was granted, in which she entertained her parents more than once. On her husband's return to Scotland (against a ransom of 100,000 marks) she at first went with him but, unable to condone his loose living, soon returned to a more restful life at Hertford. And there in 1362 she probably died, aged only 41 years – four years after her mother, Queen Isabella, who also died at the castle.

Her second sojourn coincided with the arrival of another prisoner-of-war – one whom we met at Berkhamsted, John, King of France. Accompanied by his son, a numerous suite of French nobles, royal secretaries, body servants, a minstrel and a fool, he appears to have taken captivity with an easy mind, hunting, feasting and receiving visits – a freedom which enabled him to conspire with a handful of traitorous Englishmen and necessitated his removal after only a few months to Somerton in Lincolnshire.

It was while staying at Hertford that Catherine, widow of Henry V, lost her master cook (bearing the inappropriate name of John Hunger) and buried him in All Saints church. All Saints was burned down in 1891 but the inscription at the foot of his monumental brass is still to be found on the wall of the north transept in the rebuilt church. Memorials to other royal servants of various periods were, however, destroyed.

Henry VIII made frequent use of the castle, both in his own person and in those of his various wives and children. There is evidence to suggest that he planned extensive alterations to the fabric – conversion, probably, from medieval fortress to Tudor palace – but, in spite of detailed surveys and much correspondence, few appear to have been carried out. His last visit was in 1542; thereafter it was used chiefly as the home of Prince Edward, his son by Jane Seymour, who shared it from time to time with his sisters, Mary and Elizabeth. The nine-year-old Edward was at the castle when, in 1547, his father died, though the news was not broken to him until he was on his way to London.

The castle appears to have been a favourite refuge for Elizabeth in times of plague – in 1546, 1572, 1576, 1589 and 1593; it was during one of these visits that the pargetted houses (pargetting skilfully restored in 1940) opposite the *Salisbury Arms* were built, probably as Government offices. She was the castle's last royal occupant – though there is a story, not well authenticated, that Cromwell issued from it in wrath to quell a Leveller – the levellers were an extreme left-wing group – disturbance among his own followers on Corkbush Field, between Hertford and Ware, and to shoot three of its ringleaders. Of most of its later occupants, lessees of the Salisburys, there is no occasion to speak, notable though some of them were; but in the opening years of the nineteenth century the recently renovated gatehouse and its surrounding precincts were put to a use altogether unprecedented.

As a college in which to train its future officers the East India Company installed at the castle in 1806 a number of boys of good family for a three-year course of study. The Company's original intention was to establish itself there permanently; but it soon discovered that its interests would be better served by erecting its own, and much larger, edifice on Hertford Heath, designed by William Wilkins, afterwards architect of the National Gallery – the great block that since 1862 has been the college of Haileybury. The transfer from Hertford was made in 1809, but a preparatory school continued in the gatehouse for a further nine years.

Contemporary prints show earnest students, soberly gowned and mortar-boarded, pacing its lawns in converse with turbaned Orientals or immersed beneath its trees in tomes of probably unfamiliar script while the Lea flows tranquilly in the background. And study was certainly called for; the curriculum included history, law, mathematics, military tactics and, of course, a great variety of Oriental languages. At the entrance age of 16 students must, according to a book of the period, 'possess competent knowledge of at least two Latin classics, the easier parts of the Greek Testament and the principles of grammar as well as the common rules of arithmetic, together with vulgar and decimal fractions'. The fees were 100 guineas a year, plus the cost of books and stationery, proper academical dress, 'tea equipment etc.'; and on leaving the college they had to pay ten guineas for the use of the philosophical (scientific) apparatus and the library. Yet in spite of, perhaps because of, steady grinding and grounding under such professors as the Reverend Thomas Malthus (whose theory of population, at that time revolutionary, is still arguable), the earnest students of the prints were by no means averse from ragging that verged on the sadistic, both in their own premises on Hertford Heath and in Hertford itself, which they several times painted red – indeed, on at least one occasion the College had to be closed and its students sent home. Their juniors, still at desks in the gatehouse, no doubt envied them.

One more Hertfordshire castle was in, so to speak, reputable hands throughout its life – Waytemore Castle, Bishop's Stortford, built by the first Norman Bishop of London on what, it has been argued, may have been either a large, or enlarged, tumulus or a Roman-occupied hillock beside a ford over the Stort. In the hands of the Bishops it remained for many centuries – even after it had been allowed to fall into decay in the sixteenth. What can be seen of it now is the motte, 42 feet high, oval in shape, with a summit area of some 600 square yards containing the bases of flint-rubble walls 12 feet thick. Early in this century its sides were described as having been 'much undermined and destroyed by rabbits'; I can scarcely believe that any intelligent rabbit today would choose a spot adjacent to a public garden, a large car park and a busy road – to say nothing of Urban District Council offices within easy view. For all the outer defences and immediate surroundings of the castle have been levelled in the making of amenities to the town.

Only one brief interruption occurred in its occupation by the Bishops. In 1207 Bishop William fell foul of King John over the appointment of Stephen Langton to the See of Canterbury; whereupon John seized castle and town (at that time also in the Bishop's hands), set about demolishing the former and created the latter a borough sending its own representatives to Parliament. But John was in deep waters, himself excommunicated and with England under an interdict by the Pope; not long afterwards William was authorised to rebuild his castle, John accepting the responsibility for rebuilding it. The town, which retained borough status for 150 years, remained in the King's hands. A century later Edward III licensed the Bishop of that time to strengthen his fortifications (though they were never tested in warfare) and to endow a chantry of secular priests in the castle chapel. Thereafter, as I have said, the castle fell little by little into neglect, ceasing to lodge the Bishops on their visits or even to be supervised by a Constable appointed by them. One portion, however, did not – the prison.

Exactly where the prison lay in relation to the castle itself is not clear; its use is clear enough. It appears to have housed at various times prisoners not only from Hertfordshire but also from the Bishop's estates in Middlesex, Surrey and Sussex. In 1291 no fewer than 50 prisoners were confined in it, of whom 29 died within the year and were buried close by; all were chained in irons, some to the wall, others to posts. In 1347 there were 25 prisoners, of whom nine died. Gradually, however, the numbers fell off; but during the persecution of Mary's reign Bishop Bonner revived its use with gusto, making, it was very soon afterwards recorded, 'great use of the prison adjoining the castle where he kept convicted Protestants in a deep and dark dungeon'. At least one appears to have been burned alive – no doubt to encourage the others. Yet before raising eyebrows at such dubious exhibitions of Christianity we shall do well to remember that Churchmen, then as now, were first and foremost men of their time, bound by its outlook and its codes of behaviour. The few who were not might well qualify for sainthood.

In order to understand the remaining castle sites in Hertfordshire a reminder of history is necessary – of the period when, as was then written, 'men said openly that Christ and His saints slept'.

Having no sons, Henry I, grandson of William of Normandy,

appointed as his successor his daughter, Maud, widow of the Emperor of Germany, and compelled his Barons (some much against their will) to swear fealty to her. One of those who did so was Henry's cousin and favourite, Stephen, son of the Conqueror's daughter, Adela, widow of the Count of Blois. Stephen, 22 years of age when he took the oath, had spent nearly all his life at his uncle's court but shared with many others a doubt about the ability of any woman to rule a country in times when too often might was right. On Henry's death in 1135 therefore, Stephen, who had been in Normandy, hurried over to England and, strongly supported both by an influential section of the nobility and by such important towns as London and Winchester, was crowned King.

Though undoubtedly genuine in his desire for peace and justice, he proved, however, incredibly ham-handed in his management of affairs, calling in foreign mercenaries to his aid and woefully neglecting, as a more astute man would not have done, to play off his supporting Barons against their opponents and natural rivals. After a year or two, and on behalf of Maud (who had now for long been married to Geoffrey Plantagenet), the King of Scotland invaded and was defeated; but Stephen was not sufficiently well established to push victory home, leaving much of the north of England in Scottish hands. Next he fell foul of the Earl of Gloucester, Henry 1's illegitimate son and one of the most powerful of the Barons – and then of the Church. Under the cloak of dynastic rivalry, and with Stephen's influence daily weakening, the Barons were not slow in renewing their mutual and equally bitter rivalries; anarchy descended upon England, every man at war with every other. In 1139 Maud herself landed, in due course capturing Stephen and being acknowledged Queen. But her arrogance and greed soon antagonised her friends; in 1141 she was forced to release Stephen in exchange for Gloucester, who had been taken by her opponents, and for some years a confused and merciless struggle did but perpetuate the anarchy of the preceding ones. Gradually Stephen regained much of the ground he had lost but was never able to establish effective supremacy. In 1146, however, Maud finally left England – but not before her son by Geoffrey Plantagenet, Henry of Normandy and

Anjou, had sworn to take up the fight where she had left it. A few years later he in his turn invaded; but in the meantime Stephen had lost his only son, Eustace, whom he had seen as the instrument of England's salvation. Weary and disheartened, he agreed to acknowledge Henry as his successor to the English throne. He died in 1154.

Against this bloodshed background we must pin-point one man, Geoffrey de Mandeville, grandson of a former Geoffrey to whom William of Normandy had granted many manors in Hertfordshire, Essex and elsewhere. In true gangster fashion the Geoffrey of Stephen's time adhered to whichever side promised the greatest momentary advantage, killing, burning, terrorising to gain his ends. His chief stronghold was Saffron Walden in Essex, where he had founded an Abbey – there are times when the medieval mind appears to us uncomprehensible in its apparent cynicism. He became Sheriff of Hertfordshire and Essex, of London and Middlesex, and Constable of the Tower – a force powerful enough to be able to coerce lesser landowners over a wide area into compliance with his ambitions. Through most of Stephen's reign he flourished in evil but Nemesis awaited him – after death his excommunicated body was hung in a leaden sheath outside the Temple Church in London.

An obvious act on his part was strongly to fortify the chief houses of all his key manors and to persuade his supporters to fortify theirs. One of the undertakings of Henry II on ascending the throne after Stephen was to demolish all such unauthorised, or 'adulterine', castles as had grown up in the preceding period. It is said that throughout England there were some 1,150; eight were in Hertfordshire, one in the south, three in the middle, four in the north. With so short a life, what can be seen of them today?

First, then, that of South Mimms. Lying a little west of A 6 on the lower slopes of Ridge Hill, it had become so overgrown and completely forgotten that the site was not recognised as that of a castle until 1918. In 1960, however, excavation revealed something of its nature. Constructed in the first instance by Geoffrey, it consisted of a circular motte 110 feet in diameter at the base and 65 feet at the summit but at present rising to only about 12 feet above ground level; a kidney-shaped inner bailey 300 feet across and surrounded by a moat and timber palisade; and possibly an outer bailey, of which faint traces still exist. On the motte stood a timber tower 36 feet square, with flint footings; it had a basement entered by a timber-lined tunnel through the side of the motte and its walls sloped gently inwards, like those of a windmill or lighthouse. What its height may have been is uncertain; but judging by discoveries made during excavation, its upper rooms were probably plastered internally, well-furnished and, it may be, richly decorated, while its roof was of lead.

Though the motte may have ceased to be occupied after Geoffrey's death, finds in the bailey show occupation for at least another 50 years – indeed, for longer than that – warning us against assuming that Henry II's suppression of adulterine castles was invariably followed by their immediate abandonment. It may be added that the site is now protected by the Ancient Monuments Act.

Of the three castle sites in the middle of Hertfordshire the most interesting is that at Benington, though, since privately occupied, it is difficult to inspect. Moreover, the castle remains are bedevilled by newer building in neo-Norman style. The motte, now a mere hillock, contains the flint wall bases of a square keep with sides of 40-odd feet – the only square Norman keep in the county. Part of the moat surrounding the inner bailey is some 12 feet deep and it is probable that the church was enclosed in an outer bailey, of which two ponds on the further side of the road to Hebing End were feeders to the surrounding ditch. It was Peter de Valognes, lord of the manor and adherent of the tempestuous Geoffrey, who built the masonry works to replace the timber defences erected by his father, thus being responsible for the most formidable adulterine stronghold in the region. Its effective life, however, was little more than 40 years; the Exchequer accounts for 1177 include a charge for 100 picks used in demolishing it. But how thoroughly demolition was carried out is problematical, since subsequent lords of the manor appear to have had their principal dwelling on the site. Then, in about 1745, Sir John Chesshyre, built the present house, the Lordship, inside the moat and alongside the motte; and roughly a century later not only was the house given a neo-Norman face-lift but a neo-Norman gatehouse was added, both, it is said, by a landscape gardener named James Pulham, who soon afterwards established himself as a maker of terracotta and artificial stone at Broxbourne. A general view of the site today, with church, Lordship, castle fragments, robust trees and village green in juxtaposition, is undoubtedly picturesque and is a good deal photographed but should not be looked on with too uncritical an eye.

About the other two castles, both small, very little is known. That at Walkern, built by Hamo de St Clare, another adherent of Geoffrey, does not appear to have had more than timber fortifications; all that remains of it is the ditch surrounding the bailey, the bailey itself being partly covered by the buildings of Walkern Bury Farm. At Great Wymondley, however, the castle appears to have been built not by one of Geoffrey's men but by John de Argentein, a supporter of the King – which did not apparently rescue it from demolition by Henry II. Situated just behind the church, its motte and moat can still be seen, though no evidence is forthcoming of masonry or of the inclusion of the church within its bailey. Adjoining is a ditched enclosure which, it is claimed, may have been occupied in Roman times; but, so far as I am aware, no excavation has been undertaken to prove or disprove the claim.

The four castles in the north of the county lie in an arc between Anstey, some miles north west of Bishop's Stortford, and Pirton, to the north-west of Hitchin. Though little is known of the history of any of them, their fortification or re-fortification under the pressure of Geoffrey is fairly safely to be presumed, since they may be regarded as covering his main stronghold at Saffron Walden from the south-west. It will be convenient to follow this arc from its eastern tip.

Anstey lies on a hilltop overlooking a rich valley through which flows a small stream; from the village a road dipping steeply into the valley passes Anstey Hall and the church. Behind them lies the castle, approached by a short roughish track leading to the stables of the Hall and, in the opposite direction, to farm buildings in rear of the church. Before one is the tree-covered motte, 35 feet in height, with a summit area of a quarter of an acre and surrounded by a deep moat, for the most part wet – except for that at Bishop's Stortford, the highest motte in the county. But what are not seen, since they lie in the grounds of the Hall, are a square moated barbican motte and a large bailey covering a full acre, also moated but separated by a moat from the principal motte. The bailey is divided into two portions by a scarp, one portion being some feet higher than the other; and at its south end there are traces of an embankment, probably part of outer defences that were destroyed by the present road, and that ran parallel to it, including, it may be, the church. The maximum length of the work through motte and bailey is 550 feet; the greatest width is 480 feet.

Trial excavations in 1902 produced some, though by no means convincing, evidence of masonry on the motte but none on the barbican. There the matter was allowed to rest, though interest in the site remained active. During the Second World War an American bomber crashed with its load of bombs on top of the motte; the bombs were, I believe, successfully removed from the wreckage. But the probability of encountering quantities of still live machine gun and other ammunition appears to have effectively deterred later investigators.

On the history of the site there is more conjecture than hard knowledge. Tradition says that a castle was built by Eustace of Boulogne, to whom William of Normandy granted the manor; certain it is that Nicholas de Anstie (whose political affiliations are unknown) was given licence to strengthen it – and in 1218 ordered to destroy all except the portion standing before the recent struggles. In 1225 it was in the King's hands, in the custody of the Archbishop of Canterbury; but there is no record of it in the fourteenth century, a predecessor of Anstey Hall no doubt taking its place.

One bit of tradition links it vaguely with the Stephen–Maud period – the tradition which speaks of it as having once been 'a den of robbers'. The 1902 investigators were told that during a dry summer 'about 40 years ago' there had been found at the edge of the moat two massive iron doors still apparently in position, with strong hinges and closed by a heavy bar. To open them, they were told, was forbidden by 'so it was said, Government' – more probably by the tenant of the Hall, conscious of the superstitions that persisted in the remoter parts of Hertfordshire at that time. Today, however, of the gates there is no trace – or has the moat not been dry enough to expose them? What were they? Geoffrey and his henchmen had no less a love of dungeons for their prisoners than had everybody else at that time.

Between Barkway and Reed, on the crest of the Chilterns and with a magnificent field of view, are the few traces of a castle known as Periwinkle Hill. As long ago as 1910, when the Royal Commission on Historical Monuments issued its Hertfordshire inventory, the site was described as 'almost level with the surrounding ground', though at that date the outlines of a bailey could be discerned; but 50 years of ploughing have done their work and today it takes an observant eye to distingush the tiny bump of the former motte from any other irregularity of surface. Apart from its building at some time in the early Middle Ages by the Eschallers family, lords of a manor hereabouts, nothing whatever is known of its history; nor is anything known of that of the better preserved castle site at Therfield, north-west of the church – a motte now only about five feet high and a bailey, surrounded by a dry moat, covering about an acre. Throughout the Middle Ages the manor of Therfield was held by the Abbey of Ramsay in Huntingdonshire and it is unlikely, though not impossible, that the castle was built under Abbey auspices.

By the way, at Sandon, somewhat east of that village, a mound covered by a clump of trees, about 87 feet in diameter and surrounded by a 14-foot ditch, is thought to be a motte thrown up in the early thirteenth century, though nothing is known of it as such. A century or more later a post mill was erected on it. Excavation about 20 years ago brought to light remains of the mill (one of the earliest known in England) but remained silent on any earlier use of the site.

Now the castle site at Therfield is known locally as Tuthill Close, with Tuthill Manor near by. There is another Tuthill at Pirton. Tuthill is a rendering of toot hill, look-out-hill; and that at Pirton also is the motte of its castle, 25 feet in height, with a shallow depression in its summit as though its defence had been a palisaded breast-work. It is surrounded by a moat of exceptional size, still largely wet. An inner bailey, partly moated, contains church and church-yard and a considerable area of rough meadow as well. But outside this bailey there are several more ditched enclosures, in which are scattered small ponds or dry hollows that might once have linked up into an inter-connected water defence. How far these outer en-closures were integral parts of the castle enceinte is difficult to trace; it seems just as likely that, taken as a whole, they may have formed the perimeter defences of a whole fortified medieval village. The site is, in fact, of such interest that it is protected by the Ancient Monuments Act.

A further possibility as to its origin was raised by a small exca-vation in the 1950s, which brought to light Bronze Age and early Iron Age material within the enclosed area. Along the crest of high ground about a mile south ran the Icknield Way; can the lower ground about Pirton have proved acceptable to early travellers in good weather, either as an alternative section of trackway or even as a small settlement? It is an intriguing theory; but without much more extensive exploration the history of the whole site must re-main a big puzzle.

So much, then, for Hertfordshire castles – that is, works intended primarily for warfare. But there exist other buildings which may loosely be classed with them, buildings erected for use solely as royal residences: King's Langley Palace, Royston Palace and Huns-don House, in the west, north and south-east of the county respec-tively. The association of Hatfield with royalty will be dealt with in the next chapter.

To call King's Langley Palace a building is, as a matter of fact, gross exaggeration – even in 1728 the county historian, Nathaniel Salmon, wrote of its surviving fragments that 'here the rubbish of royalty exists'. Today only a short length of flint wall with brick quoins remains near the summit of Langley Hill on the road to Chipperfield. Yet those few stones are eloquent of history.

In 1276 the manor was acquired from its former owner by Eleanor, wife of Edward I, changing its name from Chiltern Langley to Queen's Langley and a little later to King's Langley. Eleanor at first appears to have taken over the existing manor house; but soon a new 'capital messuage' surrounded by a park of about 128 acres is described in the official documents known as Close Rolls. By 1286 the whole royal family was able to stay in the just-completed palace and accounts extending over several subsequent years detail payments for additions to and decorations in it, including many 'paintings in the hall', executed, it has been suggested, to amuse the eight-year-old Prince of Wales, who kept his own establishment in its precincts – including servants, it is recorded, not above using their high station to seize for little or no payment whatever food was in local markets or even in private houses. Further amusement for the prince was no doubt afforded by a camel and a lion cub housed in the park.

On becoming Edward II in 1307 he continued to spend much of his time at Langley, together with his ill-starred favourite, Piers Gaveston, who, after being executed by the Earl of Warwick, was buried in the church of the Dominican Priory established close to the palace in 1312 after several years in a smaller house alongside the river Gade. Of this priory Edward and his successors were lavish patrons; but, like all such institutions, it was suppressed by Henry VIII and soon began to fall into decay. A small outbuilding in flint and brick, popularly known as King John's Bakehouse, survived, however; in the 1880s it was described as inhabited by pigs, fowls and a labourer's family. Early in this century it was restored and enlarged and is now part of a school.

Some accounts kept during Edward II's reign throw interesting light on the employment of Langley villagers on the royal estate – a local carpenter to make wolf traps (the heavily wooded Chilterns still harboured wolves, it seems), local boys to scare birds from crops and fruit, a man to drive beasts from park to meadows, another to look after the royal hunting dogs, a man to tend the King's armour, and so on. Moreover royalty is revealed as a considerate landlord; when crops were destroyed by a plague of rabbits peasant landholders were excused rent for their holdings, and so too when a 'murrain' hit the cattle. It may be added, by the way, that the camel appears to have been still alive, receiving hay, beans, oats and two bushels of corn a week; but of the lion cub there is no mention. By that time it would have grown into a formidable beast – perhaps too formidable to be allowed to survive.

It was under the third Edward that the palace was again enlarged, and the park also – the latter to an area of about 950 acres; some of its boundary can still be traced by, for instance, hedges of exceptional thickness and in the name of Pale Farm, close to Chipperfield Common, where it was no doubt marked by a stout wooden fence, or paling. As for the palace (though it is impossible to obtain any clear idea of its plan and little even of its size) we hear of new buildings being erected, existing ones being added to or elaborated, a great clock being installed, ironwork in considerable quantities, and 'sea coal for smelting' – a fairly early instance of the transport of coal from the crude working at Tynemouth. It is said that Queen Eleanor introduced not only carpets in place of the usual rushes but also baths – or at any rate one bath; a cistern and 'a vessel to heat the water' might give some support to the tradition.

With the birth at Langley (in 1341) of Edward III's fifth son, Edmund, the palace became involved in more dramatic history. Edward was succeeded by his grandson, Richard II, son of the Black Prince; when in 1394 Richard was in Ireland Edmund. by that time Duke of York, acted as Regent. Even then Richard had become an object of political distrust and personal hatred to an influential section of his nobles, especially to his elder uncle, John of Gaunt, Duke of Lancaster; when John died in 1399 Edmund was made Steward of England 'until Henry, Earl of Derby, shall sue for the same' – a deliberate attempt to disinherit John's son, at that time exiled to France. Whereupon Henry invaded England, where he was joined by a large part of the English nobility; Richard was taken prisoner. Shakespeare pens a moving scene in the gardens of Langley palace, in which a distracted Queen learns from a gardener that 'he is in the mighty hold of Bolingbroke' Duke of Hereford – though sober history compels the reflection that Richard's first wife, Anne of Bohemia, was dead and his second, Isabella, daughter of the French King, a child not yet in her teens; Shakespeare was not one to

18   *Tring, the Gore monument*

deprive his audience of a love interest merely because history told him to. After Richard's death at Pontefract, he was buried with little or no ceremony in the priory church at King's Langley. Three years later, in 1402, Edmund Duke of York himself was buried there in great pomp; but while Richard's tomb vanished with the rest of the priory, the tomb of Edmund is now the most conspicuous monument of the parish church.

After Edmund's death his wife, Joan, was granted the manor and with it, of course, the palace, by Henry VI – it was while she was in residence that a fire destroyed some of the buildings. Thereafter its importance as a royal residence steadily declined, it being occupied chiefly by the consorts and relatives of royalty. Nevertheless it remained in the hands of the Crown until the time of Charles I, when it was sold to Thomas Houlker of the Middle Temple.

The picturesque story of these few remaining stones has detained us a long time; we can visit Royston Palace and Hunsdon House rather more quickly.

In his southward progress from Holyrood to assume the crown after the death of Elizabeth in 1603 James I, an enthusiastic sportsman, took a great fancy to the high Chiltern heathlands around Royston. Very soon afterwards he acquired two old inns in Kneesworth Street, adding to them a series of new and spacious buildings known sometimes as the King's Lodgings, sometimes as Royston Palace. At the same time he ordered that all game should be preserved within a radius of 16 miles and appointed keepers to deal with, amongst others, scholars of Cambridge who fancied a little poaching. And here before long he found, according to a contemporary letter, 'such felicity in that hunting life that he hath written to the Council that it is the only means to preserve his health, which being the health and welfare of us all, he desires them to take the charge and burden of affairs and foresee that he be not interrupted nor troubled with too much business'.

That was all very well; but in 1605, when he was shooting quantities of little birds on Royston Heath, his Secretary of State, Sir Robert Cecil, received his first intimation of the Gunpowder Plot to

9 *Hitchin church, market in foreground*

reach official circles – a sight of the anonymous letter addressed to Lord Mounteagle (of Furneux Pelham), warning him not to attend the opening of Parliament. But such was the royal devotion to sport (or was it to health?) that two days were allowed to pass before James was informed – only just in time to assure the safety not only of Parliament but also of the King himself, who would of course have been present at the opening. It was here too that in 1618 James signed the death warrant of Sir Walter Raleigh; and he was still shooting little birds on Royston Heath a month before his own death in 1625.

Though he spent a good deal of money in maintaining roads and bridges in the neighbourhood, James and his entourage were far from popular there, judging at least from an anecdote told by a writer of the time, that one of the favourite royal hunting dogs, named Jowler, was found with a note tied about his neck: 'Good Mr Jowler, we pray you to speak to the King (for he hears you every day and so he doth not us) that it will please His Majesty to go back to London, for else the country will be undone; all our provision is spent already and we are not able to entertain him longer.'

Charles I sometimes used Royston Palace on his way to and from Newmarket; in 1642, having set out from his house of Theobalds, Cheshunt, he lodged at Royston while still vainly trying to seek accommodation with Parliament on his own terms. Four years later he lodged there again – a prisoner. But in less than a century, when it had for long been in private occupation, much of it (though not quite all) was replaced by the present eighteenth-century house with shell-hooded door and Venetian window above. Its mid-eighteenth century tenant was a lawyer named John Buxton, who is said to have died at the ripe age of 105 – it was probably he who undertook the rebuilding, though Crown rights in the property were not relinquished until 1866. From the street the Palace can, however, easily be passed without recognition of its existence.

Hunsdon lies on the road from Stanstead Abbots to Much Hadham; on a side road out of the village is Hunsdon House, incorporating part of a great moated mansion built in about 1525 by Henry

VIII on the site of an older house. A late seventeenth-century engraving shows it to have been on the E-shaped plan usually associated with the reign of Elizabeth – prophetic in a sense, since she, as well as Henry's other children, Edward and Mary, were to a large extent brought up in it. Henry himself, a great lover of Hertfordshire, was here on many occasions – once during an outbreak of sweating sickness (a type of plague) in London, when 'Laud be to Jesu', said a letter-writer of the time, 'the King's grace is very merry since he came to this house for there was none fell sick of the sweat since he came hither, and after dinner he shooteth to supper time'.

After her accession Elizabeth gave it to her cousin, Sir Henry Cary, 'whose hands were better than his head and his heart than either' and whose grandson, Sir Robert, is remembered for his astonishing ride from Greenwich to Holyrood in 60 saddle hours to acquaint James of Scotland with Elizabeth's death. It was no doubt one or other of the Carys who added elaborate curvilinear gables to the wings and an ornate clock turret; and no doubt the sickly infant, afterwards Charles I, who was in the care of Sir Robert and his wife, enjoyed fine fishing in the moat.

But in 1804, when the Cary family had given way to Nicholson Calvert, big London brewer and M.P. for Hertford borough, most of Henry's mansion was rebuilt in the picturesquely castellated and Gothic-windowed fashion of the day, so that, in Sir Nikolaus Pevsner's words, it is now 'one quarter or less of a great Tudor house'. Yet as its sixteenth-century brickwork shows, parts still remain – the angle buttresses and some of the masonry of the house itself, a gatehouse, a small summer house and some odd walling. An idea of its former size may be had from the fact that the present house is only the old north wing.

Calvert's pretty drastic modernisation was found by his wife to be 'so dreadfully expensive a job' – so at least she wrote in a diary that gives vivid (and sometimes far from complimentary) pen sketches of early nineteenth-century Hertfordshire and London society. It gives also an artless account of the local activities of a typical squire's wife. Mrs Calvert once started a village school and even for a time assisted the schoolmistress – 'but I do not mean always to do that'. In simple fact she never did it again. Instead she took to herself inoculating the villagers, her tenants, against smallpox – they dared not, of course, refuse and it was lucky for her that she escaped without tragedy. At another time she had a sudden craze to learn shoemaking and insisted upon the village cobbler teaching her. A frivolous but astute and certainly well-meaning woman, a good mother and a good wife; what harm did she do compared with the equally frivolous, equally astute but infinitely less scrupulous Henry by the Grace of God?

On the further side of Ware from Hunsdon – not far from Hoddesdon, to be precise – is another building with, in a sense, royal associations. It is the ruined gatehouse of the former large manor house of the Rye, in which was hatched in 1683 a plot to assassinate Charles I and his brother James, Duke of York (afterwards James II) as they returned to London from Newmarket by a side road that passed close to the house. One of the instigators was the tenant of the Rye, a fanatical survivor of Cromwell's army named Richard Rumbold; but it had probably already been given away by one of his confederates and was in any case frustrated by a fire in the royal lodgings at Newmarket, which brought Charles back to town some days earlier than he had planned. Official investigation revealed the existence of other plots as well and several prominent heads rolled in consequence. Rumbold himself escaped, was captured and executed at Edinburgh, and his body (or part of it) exposed on the gatehouse summit.

The original manor house of the Rye, built in 1445 and though moated never intended to be what is properly called a castle, was notable for its fine moulded brickwork (as can still be seen in the gatehouse), comparable with that of Tattersall Castle in Lincolnshire. Just when most of the house vanished is not clear; the survival of the gatehouse (much larger than it is now) may be due to its use in the eighteenth century as a workhouse for the parish of Stanstead Abbots. In about 1850 the whole site was bought by William Teale, licensee of the neighbouring inn at that time called the *King's Arms* and a popular resort of fishermen on the Lea; he developed it as a pleasure ground and amusement park soon frequented by what in those days were called the lower orders – a great deal later in the century the procession of charabancs and carts passing through Hoddesdon from London on a Monday morning used to provoke the comment, 'Here comes the rent dodgers'. Shortly before the Second World War fire destroyed a great part of the gatehouse, which for 20 more years was allowed from neglect and exposure to weather to deteriorate still further – and also, even more recently, from the vibration caused by a speedway track and roller-skating rink at its foot. At the same time part of it was a public convenience. Some attempt to arrest what must very soon have led to its complete destruction was made by voluntary labour; and it was not until 1954 that what remained was at last put under the protection of the Ministry of Public Building and Works.

One attraction of the nineteenth- and early twentieth-century amusement park was the famous Great Bed of Ware, about 11 feet square, with richly carved pillars and canopy, probably Elizabethan in origin in spite of the earlier date carved on it. It is said to have been made as a state bed for the manor house of Ware, being found later in a series of Ware inns before appearing at Rye House – where various indecorous stories concerning its use were no doubt retailed with gusto. Since 1931 it has been in the Victoria and Albert Museum.

Not a royal dwelling but a monument of royal memory should be remembered in this south-east corner of the county, which recent traffic direction has now ceased to make an uncomfortable road obstacle. It is Waltham Cross, at the junction of A 1010 and A 121 to Waltham Abbey in Essex, erected in 1291 to mark one of the 12 stopping places in the journey of the body of Eleanor, wife of Edward I, from Harby in Lincolnshire to Westminster Abbey: only four now remain, the most famous, of course, being the rebuilt Charing Cross. It has, however, been several times restored, sometimes pretty drastically, the last in 1950 after a severe shaking by bombs, and is in the care of the Hertfordshire County Council.

A chapter which began by describing Hertfordshire castles may aptly end with a mention of the household moats that are to be found for the most part on the eastern side of the county. More than 100 still exist, though it is impossible to give an exact number, since neither ploughing nor 'development' take account of them; but some idea of their frequency may be gained from the fact that half a century ago eight were at Reed, seven at Cheshunt, six at Much Hadham, five at Sawbridgeworth, four at Great Munden, Ashwell and Therfield respectively, and so on. They were constructed, probably less for defence than as compounds for animals at night, round smaller manor houses or large farms and may date from any period from the medieval to the sixteenth century. In the big majority of cases the buildings associated with them have vanished, leaving only a square oval ditch, sometimes shallow, sometimes of considerable depth, in the middle of a field or alongside a lane. The most notable of all is in woodland close to Gannock Green at Reed.

CHAPTER FIVE

Homes Stately
and less Stately

Even people who have scarcely heard of Hertfordshire have heard of Hatfield House. Certain stately homes elsewhere in England may surpass it in this way or that; but stately it remains – and Hertfordshire's stateliest. Other noteworthy houses there are in the county – North Mymms Park, Knebworth House, Gorhambury at St Albans, Ashridge near Berkhamsted, Moor Park at Rickmansworth, all exhibiting both fine architecture and interesting historical associations. But none excels Hatfield.

A previous mansion, on a site adjoining the present Hatfield House, was built by John Morton, Bishop of Ely, in 1497; at the dissolution of that monastery in 1539 it was taken over by Henry VIII, who used it, together with Hunsdon House, north of Ware, as a home for his children. During Mary's reign the young Princess Elizabeth was here and at Ashridge, virtually a prisoner; here she learned of Mary's death and her own succession – an oak in the park is said to be the one under which she sat to address her first Council. James I, however, beguiled not only by Royston but also by the sporting attractions of the great area known as Enfield Chase in Middlesex, exchanged Hatfield for the mansion of Theobalds, near Cheshunt and on the edge of the Chase, built by Lord Burghley and then owned by his second son, Sir Robert Cecil, James's Secretary of State, who was thereupon created Earl of Salisbury. The exchange concluded, Cecil pulled down three wings of Morton's (and James's) Old Palace, as it is now called, erecting instead what Pevsner describes as 'one of the four or five most important Jacobean mansions in England', therein echoing the Royal Commission on Historical

Monuments: 'One of the finest existing examples of early seven-teenth-century architecture'.

Such authorities are not to be gainsaid, even if one wished to gain-say them. Its scale is palatial, its aspect noble, its setting impressive. From the wrought-iron gates facing Hatfield station the view up the shady approach avenue whets the expectation by at first reveal-ing nothing of what lies ahead; and if, when the House does come into view, the north front appears somewhat formal (except for the magnificent central doorway) it must be remembered that, as first planned, the principal entrance was in the middle of the loggia, now enclosed as an armoury (containing among other things four Sheldon tapestries) that is recessed between the large wings of the south front. There is a tradition that in the later seventeenth century a local magnate, Sir Francis Boteler, sought to uphold a right of way, which he claimed that Cecil had violated in building where he did, by riding on horseback once a year up the steps of the north door-way, through the middle of the mansion and out by the south entrance. It may be added, by the way, that the forecourt of the north front was enlarged in 1869 – but to receive the carriages of distinguished guests, not the cars of casual visitors.

Pevsner is loud in his praises of the House and I may perhaps be allowed to quote him. Its south façade is 'a sumptuous display'. The screen adjoining the Hall is 'a spectacular display of Jacobean carving, immensely skilful and of barbaric profusion'. The Great Staircase is 'of the same superb craftsmanship'. And so on. Origin-ally, it seems, an even more splendid plan for the House was pro-jected; but Cecil was not the man to spend money unnecessarily and his account book, preserved among the Hatfield archives, shows him carefully pruning away one elaboration after another. Indeed, he plainly kept matters both great and small very much in his own hands – even to acting as his own supervisory architect, though he had some assistance from William Basyll, Surveyor of the King's Works, and a great deal more from his clerk of works, Robert Lyminge – in fact, Lyminge has been named as, if not the only, at least the chief begetter of nearly all the detailed design and con-struction; he afterwards designed Blickling Hall in Norfolk, where he died in 1628. Much of the joinery work, wainscotting and the design of chimney pieces was entrusted to a Dutchman, Janever, living in London. A French engineer laid down a complicated system of water supply from the river Lea to both House and fountains; and John Tradescant planned and planted the gardens afterwards maintained by a staff of French gardeners and including a vineyard (with vines provided by the wife of the French Ambassador) since destroyed but in its day praised by both Pepys and Evelyn.

Excellent guides conduct visitors round the House; it would be unfair to them, as well as an anticlimax for their audiences, to reveal here what they have to tell on the spot, even though they do not of course show what are indubitably the House's most treasured possessions – the Diary of Lord Burghley, recording amongst other things the whole story of the Armada as seen from Whitehall, and the Casket Letters of Mary, Queen of Scots. But two impressions derived from a visit can safely be given.

Is it intrinsic vitality of character or an historical build-up over several centuries that seems to impose a sense of the abiding presence of Queen Elizabeth in a house that, in fact, was not in existence during her lifetime, intimately though she knew its predecessor? Bitterly she knew it too – so far as I am aware, she never once returned to Hatfield after accession. Yet here she is today, quite apart from her portraits – by Hilliard, Zuccaro and Cornelius Vroon – her pedigree from Adam, a number of personal relics, including a pair of silk stockings (possibly the first to be imported into England), her hat, her garden gloves, and a painting of the white horse on which at Tilbury she inspected the troops awaiting the Armada. In the park her oak still stands. No doubt such things contribute to the impression; but there is something more. The Cecils – Lord Burghley and Sir Robert – served her well, even though the hunchback Sir Robert had to endure such nicknames as 'pigmy' and 'elf'; was it he who, in destroying most of the Old Palace, her house of cruel memories, graciously laid open to her spirit this new and happier one?

Which is not, of course, to say that Elizabeth, Queen though she was, overrides the long line of Cecils who have dwelt here from about ten years after her death to the present day. And 'dwelt' is the operative word. There are stately homes that, when one is allowed to inspect them, are more stately than homes – superb set-pieces, magnificent museums. Hatfield House makes no attempt to vie with them; the present Marquess lives principally in the east wing but an aura of domesticity pervades the whole. One feels at home here. It seems so likely that, when drugget and silken ropes have been removed after the House is closed, the chairs one has admired from afar may well be sat on by the Cecils or their guests, the tables littered with coffee cups and ashtrays, the carpets and rugs a little rumpled by their feet. One can easily hear in imagination the rise and fall of political discussions, social talk or family chit-chat; nor, looking back a little in time, is it difficult to visualise the scene sketched in Lord David Cecil's short Guide when he describes the introduction of electric light in the 1880s: 'Apart from the risk of shocks, the naked wires on the Gallery ceiling were apt to break into flame. The family sitting beneath nonchalantly threw up cushions to put the fire out and then went on with their conversation.'

Cecil portraits are, naturally, everywhere – by Kneller, Reynolds, Romney, Wilkie, Richmond and Orpen, as well as a curious one of the third Earl painted over the Duke of Monmouth, of whom he was a cautious supporter in 1685. Sir Robert, first Earl, never lived here, dying at Marlborough in 1612 on his way to take up residence for the first time; yet here it is, in the midst of his splendid creation, that his spirit triumphs. His immediate successors, however, were of indifferent quality, one of them stripping the House of its most prized possessions in order to maintain his mistress elsewhere. Only with James, seventh Earl, who was created Marquess in 1789, did rehabilitation of the family name begin.

After some initial hesitation his son, second Marquess, was among the few aristocrats in England to view the coming of railways with a toleration that was almost a welcome. When Hatfield station took shape in 1850 he constructed the present approach drive, bridging Park Street and alongside the early Georgian dower house; he also induced the Great Northern Railway Company to extend their station building in order to provide him with a private waiting room while his railway coach was being shunted into the bay adjoining. What is more, he conjured out of the pockets of the Company £8,000 towards the re-alignment of the Great North Road (A 1000) to its present course between Hatfield and Bell Bar, the previous one having cut through his park, thrust itself between church and Old Palace and descended the steep hill of Fore Street. As I write these lines a further major road change, no doubt helpful to traffic but destroying the picturesque aspect of much of the old town, is taking place.

It was, however, the third Marquess, Robert Arthur Talbot, who restored the Cecils to their former eminence by becoming three times Prime Minister – in 1885, 1886 and 1895, retiring from public life in 1902, the year before his death. This is no place to detail his political career; suffice it that throughout, in the words of *The Times* of 1903, Hatfield was the scene of 'great official garden parties with their strange congeries of Eastern statesmen, Indian chiefs and Negro kings; warriors and diplomatists; the great world of London; the little world of the country; Tory members whom it was a duty to invite and Radical members who were delighted to be asked'. Queen Victoria, the Prince and Princess of Wales, the Crown Prince of Germany (better known afterwards as the Kaiser), the Shah of Persia and potentates innumerable were present at one time or another; the last splendid function took place to celebrate the coronation of Edward VII. A more than lifesize figure of the Marquess, every inch a statesman, broods impressively over the entrance to the park from road or station; while as for his Marchioness, let the county historian, Cussans, speak in a private note: 'the nicest, homeliest, and may I say the most motherly and kissable woman that ever lived'. Was it she, I wonder, who first invited Lewis Carroll to the House in 1871? He was, at any rate, much in demand there by the Salisbury children and it was at Hatfield that he invented for their delight the story afterwards published as *Sylvie and Bruno*, containing scenes directly inspired by the surroundings in which they were conceived.

Those of us who are middle-aged or more will remember the next generation of Salisbury sons – the fourth Marquess, Minister in several Conservative Governments, who died in 1947; Lord Robert Cecil, staunch supporter of the inter-war League of Nations; Lord Hugh Cecil, a redoubtable upholder of the High Church faction of the Church of England. The present Marquess, leader of the House of Lords even before he succeeded to the title, was Minister in the Conservative Governments of 1951 and 1955; his brother, Lord David Cecil, Professor of English Literature at Oxford, needs no introduction to discriminating readers.*

Both the second and the third Marquess gave much thought to the restoration of the House, not always perhaps with the happiest results; but it was the second Marquess on whom the burden fell of virtually rebuilding the west wing (though using much old material), which had been gutted by fire in 1837. It was a fire, moreover, that had encompassed the death of his 85-year-old mother, the Dowager Marchioness Mary Amelia – certainly the most picturesque of all holders of the Salisbury title, though to her contemporaries either a powerful, if seldom lovable, figure, an object of exasperation or something of a joke. Miss Carola Oman's *The Gascoyne Heiress*, based on the diary of her daughter-in-law, gives many sidelights on her extravagance and the hopeless entanglement of her finances. The diary of the wife of a Hertfordshire M.P. (of the opposite Party), watching her excursions into the political field, declared that 'she ceased not for an instant to remember her rank and to compel others to recollect it'. Sir Robert Walpole told how she would ride about the park at Hatfield 'in a phaeton drawn by four long-tail Flanders mares. She driving the wheel horses and a postilion on the leaders, with two out-riders on corresponding long-tail blacks. Her man and maid were in the chariot behind.' Or on other days she would be rowed about the Broadwater, also in the park, in a state barge with 12 men in livery at the oars. At Newmarket she never missed a meeting. Cards, it is said, lay ankle deep in the Long Gallery at Hatfield when she had been playing the night before. And when old and virtually blind she was wont to don the blue and silver habit of the Hertfordshire Hunt (which she herself had established)

---

* Lord David Cecil is now (1970) engaged in writing a full-scale account of Hatfield and the Salisbury family.

and, with a groom at her side, lead the field. When approaching an obstacle the groom would cry, 'Damn you, my Lady, jump!' And jump she did. Pluck, recklessness, pride – which? But typical of her whole life.

Without disrespect to its more exalted occupants, it is (to me at least) with her in mind that we leave Hatfield for an almost contemporary house, North Mymms Park, about three miles to the south-west.

North Mymms Park – like Hatfield House, near the site of a previous building – was erected in about 1599 by Sir Ralph Coningsby. As we should expect from its date, it closely resembles in style its more magnificent neighbour; indeed, at first glance one might almost mistake the one for the other, though North Mymms Park has neither the size nor the rich detail that distinguish Hatfield. A fine example of its period though it may be, it is better known for its collection of pictures – by Bellini and Breughel through Canaletto, Reynolds and Lawrence to Bonington – than for its architecture.

Its predecessor had come into Coningsby hands in 1530; Sir Ralph, High Sheriff of Hertfordshire, found the cramped medieval house unworthy of his increasing wealth and exalted station. But to his son, Sir Thomas, the more pretentious mansion left him by his father proved an incubus indeed. Like Sir Ralph, Sir Thomas was High Sheriff. At the outbreak of the Civil War in 1642 that office had been abolished by Parliament, its holders everywhere being, of course, adherents of the Royalist cause. But Sir Thomas had the courage of his convictions. Early in 1643 he rode over to St Albans with his *posse comitatis* and there, in the middle of a crowded market-place, read a proclamation rallying the town to the King – knowing well enough that the county was strongly, aggressively, Parliamentarian in sympathy. He might still have returned home in safety, however, but for the chance appearance of Cromwell, recently promoted to Colonel, and a group of horsemen on their way from London to Huntingdon. A skirmish followed; Coningsby was arrested and lodged in the Tower. North Mymms Park was ransacked and his wife and 18 children turned adrift. Some seven years later he was released on payment of a crippling fine; and very soon afterwards he died. In

1658 the family sold the mansion.

Thirty years later it passed into the hands of the Duke of Leeds, better known as Charles ii's minister, Thomas Osborne, Earl of Danby – a political turncoat, one of those who later invited William of Orange to England and received his dukedom for doing it. In ducal hands the mansion remained until 1799; later it was for short periods owned by the Fulk-Grevilles and the Sibthorps (it was a member of the latter family who saw in the crowds attending the opening of the Great Exhibition of 1851 an urgent revolutionary threat) and in 1893 by W. H. Burns, whose son, Major-General Sir George Burns, Lord Lieutenant of Hertfordshire, still lives there. Only in very exceptional circumstances, however, are visitors admitted to the interior of the mansion; but the grounds, including the rose gardens laid out by William Robinson at the end of last century, are occasionally open.

Six or seven miles north of Hatfield is Knebworth House, a rather different kettle of fish from the two just described. Originally – that is, in the seventeenth century – it was built by Sir Robert Lytton round a large quadrangle and remained almost unaltered until 1811, when his collateral descendant, Elizabeth Barbara, widow of General Earle Bulwer, pulled down three sides. But it was her son, Edward Bulwer Lytton, who gave us the house we see today – wonderfully medievalised in the Victorian taste, with brick cemented over to imitate stone, sham Gothic windows, battlements to the roof, copper-capped towers at the corners, plaster gargoyles and heraldic devices galore. There is a story that one day, when Lytton was proudly displaying the house to his guests, a gardener approached, touched his forelock and pointed up to the gargoyles: 'If you please, my lord, another of them bloody monkeys has fallen down in the night.'

The interior shows a similar blend of genuine and sham. The Great Hall, for instance, is largely authentic Jacobean; but the staircase – so we are told by another Lytton, Lady Emily, wife of the architect, Sir Edwin Lutyens – is in fact made of papier mâché. Yet a visit to Knebworth is essential, if only for its associations with Bulwer Lytton, the immensely popular, in some ways the representative, novelist of his day and even now not entirely forgotten.

Handsome, well connected, fertile in imagination, prolific in output, he was the very *beau idéal* of the Victorian author. According to Dickens after a visit to Knebworth, 'he was talkative, anecdotal and droll, looked young and well, laughed heartily and enjoyed some games we played with great zeal'. Over many years he poured out books and articles for the reviews and was an eloquent speaker on many subjects. He gathered round him a brilliant coterie, including Dickens, Forster, Douglas Jerrold, Mark Lemon, John Leech, Wilkie Collins, Maclise and others. In philanthropic mood, he and Dickens concocted an elaborate scheme (finally abortive) for helping aged and indigent writers and painters; funds for it were raised by elaborate theatrical productions at Knebworth patronised by the cream of Society. His pride in his home was genuine and generous – perhaps surprisingly so when one remembers that some of the most unhappy years of his life were spent there.

His mother had been of dominant – nay, imperious – type; her will was law and her law absolute. What chance of independent development could a small Edward expect at her hands? In due course he fell in love with Rosina Wheeler, daughter of a drunken Irish Squire and a half-baked bluestocking; no doubt wisely in principle but with an ineptitude plainly due to her basic character, Barbara Bulwer expressed her disapproval by refusing to meet Rosina, cutting off his allowance and banishing him from the house – thereby, however, revealing to him in his necessity his hitherto unsuspected literary ability. Almost at once he was able to earn a reasonable income from his pen. He and Rosina married; children were born to them; but after some years of dwindling love, persistent quarrelling, outrageous scenes by Rosina and ever-mounting misery, separation became inevitable. Meanwhile Barbara Bulwer had died and Knebworth had become his. He entered Parliament; Rosina continued intermittent persecution of the by now nationally acclaimed figure until his death. There is ample evidence to show Lytton's forbearance and generosity of character in all that happened; how far, one wonders, would a different mother have absolved him from the need to exercise both?

After a lifetime of worldly success, culminating (in 1866) in a

Barony, he died in 1873, aged 70, and was buried in Westminster Abbey. His son, first Earl and a Viceroy of India, wrote verses under the name of Owen Meredith. The present owner of Knebworth is Lady Hermione Cobbold, daughter of the second Earl and wife of Lord Cobbold, former Governor of the Bank of England.

Near St Albans the great house of Gorhambury recalls memories of the man unfairly stigmatised by Pope as 'the wisest, brightest, meanest of mankind' – Sir Francis Bacon, Lord Verulam (and Viscount St Albans too), essayist, scientist, James I's Lord Chancellor. Not, however, the present great house – Bacon's Gorhambury survives only in fragment and as a ruin in the park. It had been built by his father, Sir Nicholas Bacon, Elizabeth's Lord Keeper of the Great Seal, in about 1560 and there the Queen had twice honoured him with a visit. On his death it passed to his elder son, Sir Anthony, and thence, in 1601, to his younger, Sir Francis, who enlarged it (the existing porch is part of his work), modernised the interior and in it dwelt, in the words of John Aubrey, 'as if the court were there, so nobly did he live'. After his disgrace in 1621 (on charges of corruption – but what office-holder in his day was not, to our way of thinking, corrupt?) he retired to Gorhambury for the remaining years of his life, there to produce *The Advancement of Learning*, a book of deep influence in laying the foundation of all modern scientific thought. On his death, heavily in debt, in 1626, old Gorhambury went to his cousin and secretary, Sir Thomas Meautys, who erected in St Michael's church, not far off, a remarkable monument showing him, as did so few at that time, in characteristic attitude – *sic sedebat* (thus he sat), says the inscription. A quarter of a century later the mansion was sold to Sir Harbottle Grimston, Master of the Rolls, whose descendants continued to live there in spite of its manifest defects in an age demanding a very different style of display to a very different generation of Joneses. Not until 1773 (when the Grimstons had become Viscounts and were later to become Earls of Verulam) was the decision taken to abandon it for a new and handsomer mansion designed by Sir Robert Taylor.

A good example of his work it assuredly is too, even though now lacking the low wings that once connected the main building with

two side blocks. It is approached by a handsome flight of steps under a Corinthian portico leading into the great hall, built in a cube to afford the best possible hanging space for pictures. And it is indeed those pictures that form its prime attraction, including as they do a portrait of Elizabeth attributed to Hilliard, a lifelike portrait of Sir Francis Bacon by Paul Van Somer and three out of a total of only five known works by Sir Nathaniel Bacon, Sir Francis's half-nephew, an amateur painter of considerable distinction. Ruysdael, Hals, Lorraine, Huysmans, Van Dyke, Kneller, Reynolds, Lely and others are also represented; but the highspot of the collection, a portrait of Edward Grimston, 1446, by Petrus Christus, is on permanent loan to the National Gallery. The house also contains (suitably framed and hung) the earliest known English-made pile carpet, dated 1570, and two screens containing stained glass of about 1560 from the Gorhambury of the Bacons.

In the west of the county are a couple of great edifices which, though no longer stately homes, were so to within the last half century or thereabouts and can perhaps without too much stretching the definition be included here. They are Ashridge, near Berkhamsted, and Moor Park, Rickmansworth.

While close approach is not in these days encouraged, the white 1,000-foot frontage of Ashridge can still be glimpsed among its trees from Berkhamsted Common. We owe it to the famous third Duke and sixth Earl of Bridgewater, who in the last years of his life had more than recovered from the gigantic cost of his canal projects and was at last able to spare attention for his woefully neglected ancestral home. This was, of course, the old medieval monastery founded in the thirteenth century but owned by the Egertons since 1604. In its place he commissioned James Wyatt to build anew on its site; but scarcely had he done so than he died in 1803. It was his successor, the seventh Earl, who watched its building, employing Wyatt's nephew, Sir Jeffry Wyatville, to make additions a few years later.

In a sense Ashridge and Knebworth are closely akin, each an expression of its age's medieval dream world, though in the hands of such architects as the Wyatts senior and junior, Ashridge is by far the completer realisation. Whether you like it or not is a matter of taste. To Pevsner it is 'a spectacular composition', to other competent observers 'a wedding cake' and 'like a snowman, built up by sticking on lumps instead of having good bones inside it'. What has always appeared to me slightly disconcerting is the thought of it as the home of the seventh and eighth Earls, the latter of whom maintained his family's reputation for eccentricity by dressing up cats and dogs in human clothes and seating them at his table and in his carriage. The Earls Brownlow, who inherited Ashridge from him, were of more conventional mould, benevolent Victorians who knew what was good for their tenants (or thought they did) and saw to it that 'if a tenant attends strictly to the rules' he could count on Brownlow benevolence for the rest of his life. But they had no scruple in attempting to enclose 400 acres of Berkhamsted Common, thus, when challenged by another landowner, involving themselves in both physical warfare and four years of litigation, which in the end went against them. They had, however, been more successful, probably because unchallenged, on another area of the Common a few years earlier.

In 1928 its then owner, Mr Urban Broughton, gave it to the Conservative Party as a memorial college to Bonar Law; some years later it became a non-political College of Citizenship. Except during the Second World War, when it was a military hospital, it continued to serve this vitally important democratic need; but rising costs, dwindling finances and divergent views among the Trustees brought it to an end. Since 1959 it has been a College of Management, supported by a great many firms big and small as a broadening ground for their middle and upper employees.

Permission, by the way, may sometimes be obtained by interested parties to view the fascinating horse- or donkey-operated pumping gear in the undercroft, erected when the present house was built over the 280-foot well of the medieval monastery – an elaborate cast-iron construction, with three cylinders almost out of sight below the well's rim. Replacing a wooden gear mentioned as far back as the sixteenth century, it continued to function until 1857, when Lord Brownlow built at his own expense a waterworks for the neighbouring village of Little Gaddesden and provided a main to Ashridge itself.

There can be few more magnificent Golf Club houses in all England than Moor Park, Rickmansworth. A house has stood on or very close to the site since the late fifteenth century, built by George Nevill, Archbishop of York and brother of Warwick the Kingmaker, and associated with Cardinal Wolsey and with Sir William Temple and Dorothy Osborne, who spent their honeymoon there in 1655. James, Duke of Monmouth, rebuilt it shortly before his fatal rebellion in 1685; and in 1720 it was sold by his widow to Benjamin Hoskin Styles, winner of an immense fortune in the South Sea Bubble – it is said that only a day or two before the crash he received a tip from his brother-in-law, Sub-Governor of the Bank of England, to sell out while he could. Success, it may be, went to his head. No less than £130,000 – a sum today running into well over a million – went into his grandiose rebuilding of the mansion, probably designed by Giacomo Leoni in the Palladian style and with an interior, decorated by Sir James Thornhill and others, on an equally magnificent scale – though both had to sue him for payment of their fees. Two wings consisting of colonnades connecting, one a chapel, the other domestic offices, with the main building were demolished in 1785 by an owner who, unlike Styles, found himself in straitened circumstances.

Yet even without them the question imposes: where is there a 'nineteenth' to surpass it?

One act of Styles is unexpectedly commemorated. When laying out his park, the removal of an entire hill attracted the attention of Pope, who commented in his *Moral Essays*:

> *Or cut wide views through mountains to the plain,*
> *You'll wish your hill a sheltered seat again.*

In a footnote Pope explains that 'This was done in Hertfordshire by a wealthy citizen, by which means, merely to overlook a dead plain, he let in the north wind upon his house and pasture, which were before adorned and defended by woods.'

But Pope was wrong; Styles secured for himself a charming view over the Chess valley. A good deal of his park, by the way, has now been residentially developed with an opulence that the lucky speculator in South Sea affairs would no doubt have approved; but 350 acres of it are golf courses.

Styles died in 1732; a rather later owner was George, Lord Anson, Admiral of the Fleet and First Lord of the Admiralty, circumnavigator of the globe between 1739 and 1744, who died here in 1762. For much of the nineteenth century it was owned by the Marquis of Westminster and his son, the first Lord Ebury. On the death of the third Lord Ebury in 1921 the mansion became unoccupied but, together with the bulk of its estate, was bought in 1937 by the Rickmansworth Urban District Council.

Five stately homes in a county as small as Hertfordshire is no bad tally; time was when the number could be doubled. In Watford stood Cassiobury, seat of the Earls of Essex, demolished in 1927; in St Albans Holywell House, home of the Duke of Marlborough and 'Viceroy Sarah' before the building of Blenheim, gave way to road improvements 90 years earlier, in 1837. Near Hertford, Panshanger, built by Earl Cowper about 1800 to replace an earlier seat at Cole Green, was taken down in the 1950s. At North Mymms the mansion of Brookmans, built by William III's minister, the great constitutional lawyer, Lord Somers, was burned to the ground in 1891. And its neighbour, Gobions, once the home of Sir Thomas More, with eighteenth-century gardens of wide fame, vanished in 1836, only a sham medieval gateway, built about 1750, at Little Heath now surviving.

But far more numerous in the county are the houses of its erstwhile squires and lords of the manor. There are scores of them, sometimes imposing residences in a considerable park, sometimes farms, sometimes so undistinguished that they can be passed with very little, if any, notice. The majority are eighteenth-century replacements of, or embellishments to, earlier houses, often enlarged or restored in the nineteenth. Yet their common origin as the manorial foci of their localities may be deduced from the name they bear in Hertfordshire – the Bury, having the same derivation as 'borough', a fortified place. Occasionally – as at Thorley, for instance – a moat, or traces of a moat, can still be seen partly surrounding them. Today, however, organisations of diverse kinds, schools and the like, commercial firms and so on have taken over many, leaving only a few in the occupation either of wealthy individuals not of local origin or of prosperous farmers with other irons in the fire as well.

Since we have lately been looking at Ashridge and Moor Park it will be convenient to note a few large but lesser houses in that region.

One of the finest is Tring Park, built in the reign of Charles II to the design of Wren, though only his stables remain. Later in the possession of Sir William Gore, first Director of the Bank of England, and his descendants, it and its 400-acre estate were bought in 1872 by Lionel Nathan de Rothschild, who enlarged and partly rebuilt it; in Rothschild hands it continued until 1938, when most of the estate was sold piecemeal to tenants, the Hertfordshire and Buckinghamshire County Councils buying a large area of woodland for preservation. The mansion is now owned by the British Museum, Natural History Section, who also own in Tring itself the well-known natural history museum housing part of the vast collection of Lionel Walter, second Baron Rothschild – who, by the way, used to ride about the estate in a little trap drawn by three zebras and a pony; at one time by cassowaries. But after one had attacked his father cassowaries were forbidden.

As examples of justice and liberality the Rothschilds are still remembered by their former tenants, by owners of businesses retrieved by them from disaster, by the local authority and not least by poachers. 'It can be understood', comments a local writer, 'that the best minds in Tring have not sympathised with any persecution of the Jews.' Nor, would it seem, did the parson who, after receipt of much Rothschild hospitality, was frowned upon by his Bishop for consorting with non-Christians. 'But my Lord', came his bland reply, 'I have great hopes of converting them.'

Some miles east of Tring the Bury at Flamstead (actually near Redbourn) is now a farmhouse. Near Flamstead also is the mansion of

Beechwood in a small park, dating for the most part from the early eighteenth century (with additions possibly by Sir John Soane) and the home for many generations of the Saunders family and their allies, the Sebrights, whose tombs are in the church. Originally on the site of a medieval priory, it is now a school. In 1808 Sir John Sebright promoted a great fight in Beechwood Park between Bob Gregson and John Gully, Gully winning after 27 rounds lasting an hour and a quarter and incidentally amply restoring Sir John's fallen fortunes. In spite of the illegality of prize fighting at that period, 'the crowd', it is said, 'was so great that the report gained ground that the French had landed and the volunteers were called out'. But Sir John was a magistrate; no proceedings followed. Not far away, near Markyate Street, stands Markyate Cell, rebuilt about 1840 on the site of a former and much larger house of 1539, which in its turn replaced a small nunnery on the site of an anchorite's cell. In the early seventeenth century the house was occupied by a young widow named Katherine Ferrers, whom tradition asserts to have turned highwayman – a romantic version of her story was filmed in the late 1950s and proved very popular; and a public house on No Man's Land Common near Wheathampstead, where she is said to have received her fatal wound, has recently been renamed *The Wicked Lady*. Inevitably she was believed to have haunted her old home and so strong was the belief that, when the house came to be rebuilt, no local man could be induced to take a hand in it and London labour had to be called in.

On the edge of Chipperfield Common, the Manor House of King's Langley is now a block of flats. Its strangest owner in the past was, according to the always quotable Cussans in his own copy of his History, a farm labourer 'literally taken from the plough to become lord of the manor', unable to write his own name and 'too old, he said, to be a gentleman when he began to learn the trade'. John Parsley, inheriting from his uncle, took possession in the 1820s, when he was already middle-aged; living with his wife in one room he allowed only an aged servant inside the house. But as a landlord 'he would swear roundly at a poor tenant if he did not pay his rent and threaten him with all sorts of legal pains and penalties, and at night would quietly drop a £5 note under his door'. His tomb can be seen at Chipperfield churchyard.

Also in the parish of King's Langley but overlooking Hunton Bridge is the early Georgian mansion of Langleybury, built by Sir Robert Raymond, Lord Chief Justice, who died in 1732. It is now in the occupation of the Hertfordshire County Council. Almost alongside but in the borough of Watford is The Grove, a red brick mansion with stone quoins built by Sir Robert Taylor in 1756 for the Earl of Clarendon. Its most curious feature, however, is a graceful very early nineteenth-century bridge in its park over the Grand Union Canal, so steeply humped that traffic lights have been installed to both approaches. Perhaps the fact that the house is now the Motor Driver's Training School of British Railways accounts for them.

Three houses in the south of Hertfordshire claim passing attention, though only one is open to the public. They are Tittenhanger near London Colney, Salisbury Hall near Shenley and Theobalds at Cheshunt.

Tittenhanger – 'the wooded slope of Tida', according to the place-name experts, though the immediate countryside is as flat as a pancake – was built about 1630 by either Peter Mills or Inigo Jones (and incidentally containing a fine staircase by Grinling Gibbons) on the site of an ancient retreat of the Abbots of St Albans. On the dissolution of the Abbey in 1539 the older house came into the possession of Sir Thomas Pope, founder of Trinity College, Oxford; after his death without issue (though he was three times married) it passed in course of time to the nephew of his third wife, who thereupon assumed the name of Pope Blount. This nephew's son, Sir Henry Pope Blount (builder of the present house), was well known to his contemporaries as a traveller in the East; Evelyn in his Diary calls him 'the famous Traveller and Water Drinker', a reputation upheld in part by the intriguing John Aubrey, who notes that 'drunkenness he much exclaimed against, but wenching he allowed' : more spicily, Aubrey adds that he was once 'called to the Bar for spreading abroad the abominable and dangerous doctrine that it was far cheaper and safer to lie with common wenches than with ladies of quality'.

Of great interest both in itself and in its association is Salisbury

Hall, only a couple of miles from Tittenhanger. Built on a medieval moated site in the days of Henry VIII, it was in part rebuilt by Sir Jeremiah Snow (whose tomb is in Shenley church) at the very end of the seventeenth century but still shows much Tudor brickwork in rear, though its rich interior is for the most part Snow's. Nell Gwyn, when she visited the older house with Charles II, lived in a small lodge alongside a bridge over the moat; the story runs that, angered at his being granted no title, she held their firstborn, Charles Beauclerk, at arm's length over the water, withdrawing him only on Charles' horrified cry, 'Nelly, Nelly, don't kill the Duke of St Albans'. Later occupants included Lady Randolph Churchill, often visited by Sir Winston in his youth, and in the early 1930s Sir Nigel Gresley, the locomotive engineer. Here it was in the first days of the Second World War that the prototype of the famous Mosquito aircraft was designed and built – it is still on view there. And finally, Nell Gwyn's lodge is now a most intriguing silk worm farm, which has produced silk for two Coronations and a royal wedding and is conducted by Lady Hart-Dyke. House and farm are open to visitors during the summer.

It is a long journey from Shenley to Cheshunt, worth making only by the dedicated sightseer – and even then for associations rather than for what he sees. Of Lord Burghley's magnificent palace of Theobalds (pronounced Tibbalds), built about 1564 and exchanged by his son for James I's palace at Hatfield, only one strip of brickwork, now the wall of a gardener's cottage, remains. Several houses were erected on its site, none of which survives. The present Theobald's Park, about a mile away, was built in 1763, added to in the nineteenth century and again in Edwardian times. Now a school owned by the Great London Council, it was for many years the home of the Meux family, well-known brewers; in 1888 Sir Henry Bruce Meux transferred Wren's Temple Bar, which until ten years previously had stood at the top of Ludgate Hill, to his park, where it still stands in, alas, deplorably neglected surroundings, accessible to the walker but scarcely to the motorist. Also associated with Theobalds is Dr Isaac Watts, who wrote not only 'O God, our help in ages past' but also 'How doth the little busy bee', ''Tis the voice of the sluggard' and other verses now derived but worth taking to heart nevertheless.

North of Ware, Blakesware, near Widford, was built only in 1878; but its predecessor, 'Blakesmoor, in H——shire', demolished in 1823, will be familiar to every reader of Lamb as the house in which his grandmother, Mary Field, was housekeeper, and which he knew so well during his childhood. 'A strange passion for the place possessed me in those years', he wrote, endowing him in imagination with its true ownership as against those who 'had long forsaken the old house of their fathers for a newer trifle'. Walter Plumer was the name of its legal owner, belonging to a long-established county family; he had moved to New Place, Gilston, now called Gilston Park. It is perhaps a bit of poetic justice in which Lamb would have delighted that a quarter of a century later sheriff's officers invaded New Place and sold it, lock, stock and barrel over the head of the last Plumer.

West of Hertford along B 158 is Bayfordbury, a fine mansion built about 1760 by Sir William Baker, who had been employed in raising Government loans during the Seven Years' War: it is said that, when offered a baronetcy, he replied that he preferred only a knighthood 'for that confined the folly to himself and entailed no ridicule on his descendants'. The Baker family continued to live there down to 1939; during the Second World War it was in military occupation, afterwards taken over by the John Innes Horticultural Institution and more recently by the Hatfield College of Technology. During Baker occupation it housed the famous Kit-Cat portraits by Kneller, now in the National Portrait Gallery. A long mile further along B 158, Woolmers was rebuilt in his last years by the Duke of Bridgewater (who died in 1803) when he was contemplating an extensive canal enterprise (finally abortive) based on the Lea and Stort and embracing all the eastern counties.

Threading by-ways northwards from Woolmers we come to Queen Hoo Hall, Tewin, a handsome red brick Elizabethan house containing contemporary murals but not, unfortunately open to the public. Its name is stated to derive from 'Cwenhild's haga', or enclosure; but Hoo also signifies 'high ground' and Queen Hoo, on the spur of a hill overlooking a magnificent southward landscape, is certainly an appropriate adaptation of the original name.

On the other side of Tewin village is Tewin Water, the present house dating from 1798 and a century later the home of Cecil Rhodes' associate, Otto Beit, and his son, Sir Alfred, who died in 1940; it is now a Hertfordshire County Council school. But it was the previous house that saw one of Hertfordshire's most fantastic figures. She was Elizabeth Malyn, daughter of a London brewer, who married in succession James Fleet, lord of the manor of Tewin (died 1733), Colonel Sabine also a Tewin man (died about 1738), and Lord Cathcart (died 1740). She is said to have declared in later life that 'the first was to please my parents, the second for money, the third for a title and the fourth because the Devil owed me a grudge'.

The fourth, whom she married in 1745, was a young Irish adventurer, Hugh Macquire, with a castle in Maynooth and both eyes on her fortune. The more unscrupulously – and brutally – he tried to wrest it from her the more sturdily she resisted; after a year of marriage he kidnapped her to his Irish castle, keeping her in strict confinement for 20 years with only a single attendant to care for her. Then – luckily – he died, probably in a duel; in her early seventies his widow returned to Tewin and devoted the next quarter of a century to making up for all the enjoyment she had missed in the preceding one – 'it is woeful', wrote Horace Walpole, who saw her dancing in 1786, 'to have a colt's tooth when other folk have none left'; and a year later her neighbour, Earl Cowper, is said to have taken out an annuity on her life very cheaply because she had just given up dancing. She died and was buried at Tewin in 1789, in her ninety-eighth year.

The story of her fourth marriage, by the way, is fictionised in Maria Edgeworth's *Castle Rackrent*. Since Maria lived at Northchurch, near Berkhamsted, she was no doubt well informed by current gossip, if not from the old lady herself.

From Tewin it is not difficult to reach Watton-at-Stone by way of Datchworth Green; and at Watton is Woodhall Park, on the hillside east of A 602; it is now a school. Replacing a mansion that had been occupied by the same family for 400 years, it was built in

777 by Sir Thomas Rumbold out of a fortune made (none too
scrupulously, rumour alleged) in the service of the East India Company; after his death in 1791 it was bought by an even more doubtful Nabob, Paul Benfield. According to Philip Woodruff's *The Men
Who Ruled India*, Benfield had 'been dismissed the service after
six years, reinstated, suspended, reinstated a second time, suspended
and sent to London to answer charges, reinstated a third time, and
finally dismissed 18 years after he had joined, with a fortune of
half a million'. By 1805 he was bankrupt, Woodhall Park being sold
to a banker, Samuel Smith, whose descendants, the Abel Smith
family, continued to live there until recent years. The mansion is
notable chiefly for a room entirely lined by eighteenth-century
prints surrounded by paper frames engraved and tinted to imitate
gilt ones.

It is a cross-country but quietly picturesque journey from Watton
to Standon, at the extreme south of which lies Standon Lordship,
mostly rebuilt in the nineteenth century but containing fragments
of the great house of Sir Ralph Sadleir, a man of humble origins,
entrusted by Elizabeth with delicate diplomatic missions and reputed
to be the richest commoner in England. Elizabeth condescended to
stay here, and so did James I on his progress from Holyrood to
assume the crown. Inherited in due course by Lord Aston of Tixall
in Staffordshire, it became the brilliant focal point of Hertfordshire
county society; but later inheritances produced so many family
quarrels that by 1809 it had been, in the words of Sir Walter Scott's
diary, 'almost completely demolished'. In 1840, however, it was
bought by the Duke of Wellington; it was his son, the second Duke,
who rebuilt it as the house we see today, handsome and beautifully
set in the quiet remoteness of the Rib valley.

From Standon it is a fairly direct run through the hamlet of
Bromley to Much Hadham, the most photographed and most opulent
village in Hertfordshire. At its north end, near the church and backed
by a wooded hillside, is the old Palace of the Bishops of London, who
held the manor for close on a 1,000 years. Most unpalatial in appearance, its timber frame has been encased in seventeenth-century
brick and with eighteenth- and nineteenth-century additions. At

129

various times a girls' school and a private lunatic asylum, it is now flats. Not far away is the much more striking Lordship of 1720; halfway down the village street is the Hall of ten years later; and at the south end Moor Place, in large grounds, dates from 1775. If I dismiss Much Hadham somewhat curtly it is not for lack of appreciation of any of these houses, or of the many smaller properties of real architectural quality that it contains, but in order to hurry on to Little Hadham Hall, with equal but less generally popularised claim to attention.

Built round a courtyard in 1575 on the site of an older house, Little Hadham Hall was later in part demolished, only one wing (containing a fine entrance door flanked by octagonal turrets) surviving. There is also, however, some very tactful modern building, erected at about the time when it became a Hertfordshire County Council school, and a few fragments of the pre-1575 house. Here in the seventeenth century lived Arthur, Lord Capel, outspoken champion of the people in their grievances against Charles I. But on the outbreak of the Civil War basic loyalty led him into the Royalist camp. As an apparent turncoat he became in consequence anathema to the Parliamentarians, was captured at Colchester and eventually executed by them – 'murdered for his loyalty to King Charles the first', says his tablet in the church. His son, also Arthur, was created Earl of Essex by Charles II and moved his seat to the now demolished Cassiobury at Watford.

Only a short distance north of Little Hadham is Furneux Pelham Hall, seventeenth-century with curvilinear (formerly stepped) gables, where Lord Mounteagle received the mysterious letter which led to the discovery of Gunpowder Plot.

In the extreme north of the county are two houses, very different in their points of interest, that are worth mentioning. The first is Ashwell Bury, remodelled by Sir Edwin Lutyens in the 1920s; the second is Hinxworth Place, described by Pevsner as 'one of the best preserved fifteenth-century stone (clunch) manor houses of Herts', earlier a cell of Cistercian monks from Pipewell, Northamptonshire.

The last leg of our tour takes us through the middle of Hertfordshire – through Rushden, where the eighteenth-century Julians is surrounded by delightful gardens, and Cottered, with its moated fifteenth- and seventeenth-century Lordship, to Ardeley and its Bury, for the most part a strange Gothic fantasy of 1820 but embodying portions of a Tudor structure. It was in this Tudor house that there lived the county's first historian, Sir Henry Chauncy, whose *Historical Antiquities of Hertfordshire* was published in 1700. A non-historian who chances upon the book will find it worth dipping into for its engravings (in most cases, the earliest extant) of many big houses in the county as they were at that date, and also for its pen portraits of squires whom Chauncy had known personally – Edward Gardiner of Thundridge, for instance, whom he describes as 'endowed with great Modesty, Discretion and Patience, which his wife did often exercise'.

These pen portraits lead us to another aspect of the work. The Civil War of 50 years earlier had brought about the downfall or impoverishment of many of the county gentry, whose estates were sold to, for the most part, London merchants anxious to set up as country gentlemen. It was to these newcomers, wanting 'to know the privileges of their several manors', purse-proud but unversed in the best traditions of county aristocracy, that Chauncy addressed himself in his pen portraits of their predecessors, subtly depicting what they should live up to. In short, county history though it ostensibly was, the book was alive with contemporary social purpose.

A curious bit of personal history as well emerges in it. Throughout the years of its preparation Chauncy encountered the bitter opposition of his son, Henry, and of Henry's father-in-law, Sir Nicholas Butler, who put every obstacle in his path and even took him to law on a plea of illegitimately expending his son's patrimony. What kind of man Butler may have been otherwise I have no idea; according to an annotator who knew him, he 'died in his own bed as much against his own expectations as other men's'. Chauncy's rather pathetic reference to the affair in his Preface – ''tis in vain studiously to conceal what almost every Body knows' – is echoed in the body of the book whenever the historical narrative gives an opening to inveigh against 'young men who condemn their Parents and covet their Death, that they may gain their Estates before the time God hath appointed'. And on a surviving page of his manuscript, now in Hertfordshire County Record Office, occurs a note to the printer: 'I will not have my son's marriage incorporated, for my Friends and Relations have so great an Antipathy to it that I dare not own it in respect of the Mischief that will attend me by it.'

At Hitchin the Priory, a fourteenth-century Carmelite house, part of whose cloisters are incorporated in the present imposing late seventeenth- and eighteenth-century mansion, is now a Hertfordshire County Council school. May I, as my readers would no doubt wish me to, pay tribute to that fine body for its work in making use of architecturally or historically valuable buildings for educational purposes? Until recent years the Priory was the home of the Radcliffe and Delmé-Radcliffe families, Levant merchants of long standing. Some miles to the south-east, near Whitwell, St Paul's Waldenbury is the birthplace of Queen Elizabeth, the Queen Mother, in 1900 and the scene, rather more than a century earlier, of the ordeal of Mary Eleanor Bowes-Lyon, daughter of Georges Bowes of Streatlam Castle, Durham (where the Bowes Museum now is), and widow of John Lyon, ninth Earl of Strathmore, Baron Glamis, who on marriage assumed the additional name of Bowes. For like Lady Cathcart of Tewin she ventured upon further marriage – and again like her, with an Irishman, Andrew Robinson Stoney, intent on her fortune. The pattern of her ill-treatment at his hands was almost exactly similar, abduction and all; but in Lady Strathmore's case she was rescued before long by the Bowes' tenantry and Stoney afterwards convicted and imprisoned. A divorce followed. In 1800 Lady Strathmore died and was buried in Westminster Abbey; her husband, surviving her by ten years, died in a debtor's prison.

Just behind St Paul's Waldenbury, by the way, is Stagenhoe, a large eighteenth-century mansion occupied in the 1880s by Sir Arthur Sullivan while he was composing the music of *The Mikado*. He is said to have outraged local susceptibilities by filling the house with chorus girls on Sundays.

Two famous Prime Ministers lived and died at Brocket Hall, near Hatfield, a splendidly situated mid-eighteenth century mansion

above a lake formed by the Lea and best seen from the Hatfield–
Wheathampstead road, B 653. Here it was that Lord Melbourne
played out much of the distressing drama of his marriage with
Caroline Ponsonby – better known as Lady Caroline Lamb – and
spent the last years of his life, forgotten by the brilliant Society he
had for so long adorned. On his death in 1848 it passed to his
brother-in-law, Lord Palmerston, who himself died here in 1865. A
later occupant was Lord Mount Stephen, builder of the Canadian
Pacific Railway. It is now luxury flats. In its estate, but nearer
Wheathampstead, Waterend House is the birthplace of Sarah Jennings, Duchess of Marlborough, a picturesque seventeenth-century
brick and stone house alongside a ford over the Lea. One of its
former barns has been transported to St Albans, where it is a
restaurant.

Finally Harpenden presents us with two houses of interest. At a
little distance to the north-east, Mackery End, a handsome brick
house with curvilinear gables, dates from 1666; but Lamb's
'Mackery End in Hertfordshire' describes the adjacent farm (now
refaced) in which lived his kinsmen, the Gladmans. On the outskirts of Harpenden itself the seventeenth-century Rothamsted has
been incorporated into the world-famous Rothamsted Experimental
Station, conducting research into soil, plant nutrition and plant
pathology, originating in the 1830s with Sir John Bennet Lawes (later
joined by his partner, Sir John Gilbert) whose ancestors, the Witte-
wronges, built the house.

CHAPTER SIX

To the Glory
of God

In the footsteps of a multitude of medieval pilgrims from kings to peasants, it is inevitable that, to begin with, we should visit the former Benedictine Abbey of St Albans, now, of course, a Cathedral, like them to mingle genuine reverence with a lot of sightseeing. Some of the things that they saw we can see too, though a good deal more that surrounds us dates from after their time. Whether the edifice may be considered better or worse than in their day I hope to discuss shortly. But in one respect at least we have a solid advantage over them – shelves full of books, essays, histories, pamphlets, architectural surveys, drawings, prints and photographs have grown up in the intervening centuries to substitute for their unsophisticated wonder an informed appreciation. Indeed, so much has been written about the Abbey – no Hertfordshire person refers to it as anything else – so much is readily available either on the spot, in bookshops or in libraries, that nothing more seems called for here than reminders of a few facts sometimes overlooked.

First, then, a word as to the historical background. What we are about to visit was not merely the premier Abbey of medieval England, whose Abbots took precedence over virtually every other English ecclesiastic, but also the heart of a Liberty, composed of all the manors in the Abbey's possession (more than a score, and many of them large, in Hertfordshire alone), in the government of which the Abbots exercised absolute control, to the exclusion even of the King. This Liberty continued in being as an area of civil government after the Abbey's dissolution in 1539 – a county within a county, so to speak – until as recently as 1874, appointing its own Justices of the Peace (St Albans does so still), maintaining its own

22 *St Albans Abbey from the south-west*

23 *St Albans Abbey, shrine of St Alban*

gaol in the great Gatehouse and, in 1840, establishing its own police force. For all the obvious difficulties and confusions arising from this duplication of governing bodies, it had taken more than a quarter of a century of bargaining to bring Liberty and County together. Three years later, in 1877, the See of St Albans, covering Hertfordshire and Bedfordshire, was created and the Abbey, for 300 years a mere parish church, raised to the status of a Cathedral.

While in modern estimation one outstanding importance of the medieval Abbey was as the home of such notable chroniclers as Roger of Wendover, Matthew Paris and Thomas of Walsingham, the medieval saw it both as a house of God and also, and not less forcibly, as something inordinately rich, inexorable in its demands, grasping in its dealings, harsh and overbearing to and often at loggerheads with its numerous tenantry. There was certainly some justification for this view – was it not a centre of the Peasants' Revolt in 1381? Yet in spite of its enormous wealth, the misguided expenditure and wanton extravagance of Abbot after Abbot kept it continuously poor, seduced as they were by the highly aristocratic patronage that both it and its pilgrimage enjoyed, due to its easy access from London. Little might, on the whole, be said against the more obvious morals of the monks; yet here, as D. J. Hall points out in the *English Medieval Pilgrimage*, was an institution far more worldly than spiritual – 'there is less here of saintly inspiration or holy purpose than may be found in almost any other great centre of pilgrimage'. In brief, the shows and tushes of power, the glitter of prestige, the vanity of riches, gravely tarnished those aspirations to the fostering of which it had been established.

It was, of course, to the shrine of England's protomartyr, St Alban, that the Abbey owed its foundation by King Offa in 793, its fame and its popularity, aided from time to time, it may be, by practices that, despite Bernard Shaw's dictum that a miracle is an event that creates faith, we may prefer to regard as deceptions, though with no doubt a meritorious aim. The shrine in the Presbytery it was, therefore, that became and remains hallowed by the simple piety of the thousands who prayed at its foot; of all that the Abbey today

4   Sarratt, the saddleback tower
5   Detached tower at Standon
6   Hemel Hempstead tower and spire
7   Stanstead Abbots, St James's Church

contains, all its splendours, all its treasures, it is the shrine that moves one most, as the channel through which generation after generation of men, credulous yet genuine in their worship, came nearest to their God. The modern visitor sees only the richly carved marble pedestal that was erected on this spot a little after 1300, destroyed at the Dissolution and found in several thousand pieces embedded in a wall in 1872. The gorgeous feretory, which stood above it and contained the Saint's principal relics, is still lost – tradition says it was spirited away to France. Other relics were exhibited in the Watching Chamber close by.

In the Watching Chamber one or more monks guarded the shrine by day and night, exercising supervision of the pilgrims at their devotions, perhaps expatiating unctuously on the relics displayed but carefully guarded behind wooden grills, moving on dawdlers who blocked the way for newcomers – on and around 22 June, the day of the Saint's festival, one can imagine the whole area of the Presbytery nearly as thronged as a London Tube station during the rush hour. Oak-built, and dating from about 1400, it is of two storeys, the upper overhanging the lower and approached from the outside by a narrow staircase. The display cabinets (if one may call them such) on the ground floor are, in addition to their grills, furnished with stout wooden shutters, in one of which is a slit through which money might be dropped to the glory of St Alban; and on the horizontal beam that carries the front of the upper storey are spirited carvings representing, as well as the life and passion of St Alban, the procession of the months, interspersed with intriguing scenes of rural life. Of such a Watching Chamber, says Pevsner, there is only one other example – in Christ Church, Oxford.

Closely associated in all medieval minds with the veneration of St Alban was that of St Amphibalus, who is said to have converted him to Christianity and to have covered him with a cloak on his way to martyrdom. Amphibalus, the story goes, was martyred soon afterwards. Now Amphibalus is no more than the Greek word for cloak; as for the Saint himself, was there in truth any such person despite the claim (quite genuinely made) of a twelfth-century Abbot to have dug up his bones in Redbourn? He had been guided to them

he said, in a vision by St Alban. At any rate, the bones were translated with much pomp to the Abbey and duly enclosed in a handsome tomb also overlooked by the Watching Chamber. Later more
relics, even including a fragment of the cloak, were displayed. But
however sceptically historians are now inclined to view his traditional story, it will be salutary to remember once again our own
largely uncritical acceptance of many of the claims of modern
scientists, the arch-priests of this age and no more infallible than
those of old. Throughout the Middle Ages the two Saints, Alban and
Amphibalus, were linked in a single wholehearted, uncritical veneration, which concentrated itself at this spot where their tombs stood
in close proximity.

And where, in the Abbey's holy of holies, they exercised their
powers of healing, performed miracles, comforted the perplexed,
brought joy to the sad, it seemed not at all presumptuous that other
notables, though very far from worthy of canonisation, should
lie also. So it comes about that the Abbey's most magnificent tombs
in magnificent chantry chapels are at hand – those of Abbot John of
Wheathampstead, who died in 1464, and of Abbot John Ramryge,
who died in 1521; or the equally magnificent tomb of Humphrey,
Duke of Gloucester (died 1447), founder of the Bodleian Library,
Oxford, and the Duke referred to in the phrase 'dining with Duke
Humphrey' for going on short commons. In the chapel of John of
Wheathampstead is the famous brass of Abbot John de la Mare (died
1369), probably of Flemish workmanship but now so worn that it
may be rubbed by brass rubbing enthusiasts only with the sanction,
practically never given, of the Cathedral authorities. Nearby too is
the mid-fourteenth-century High Altar screen, comparable with that
at Winchester alone, though its figures are late nineteenth-century
ones; and at the east end of the nave is the late-fourteenth-century
rood screen. And in the nave itself one can scarcely fail to admire
the twelfth- and thirteenth-century wall paintings, most expertly
restored during the 1960s, on the Norman columns; but wall paintings
can be seen also in other parts of the building, as well as a remarkable heraldic display on the nave roof, probably the last embellish-
ment undertaken before the Abby's dissolution.

These notes would, however, be woefully incomplete without coming nearer to our own time, in the person of Sir Edmund Beckett, later Lord Grimthorpe. Whatever one thinks of his work, it is probably due to him that there is an Abbey still to visit.

Or is that quite accurate? Neglect over the centuries since the Dissolution certainly reduced it to a deplorable condition. At least one principal wall was badly out of the perpendicular and others were on the verge of collapse – some had collapsed already. The west front was almost in ruins, with two of its three porches bricked in. Stones were falling and mortar crumbling. There was a right of way across the nave and the Lady Chapel was occupied (down to 1867) by the boys of St Albans School. The building had been patched here and there, though nothing more, in the 1830s. But when all has been said, the state of the fabric as a whole is difficult to determine – conflicting versions were current when, in 1871, Sir George Gilbert Scott was appointed to undertake its thorough restoration.

In 1874 the Restoration Committee, formed 20 years earlier from among local landowners, ecclesiastics and antiquarians and permanently short of the requisite funds (after all, the Abbey was then still no more than a parish church), was joined by a newcomer to St Albans, Sir Edmund Beckett, brilliant Q.C., amateur horologist (he was responsible for the making of Big Ben, both clock and bell), amateur architect – and millionaire. By the date of Scott's death in 1878, which left the bulk of the work unstarted, it was plain that, in spite of opposition based on recent experience of his methods and character, Sir Edmund had made up his mind. The full story is told in Peter Ferriday's lightly handled but excellent Life of this ruthless, cantankerous, self-willed, inexhaustible and altogether amazing Baronet; two years later he obtained a Faculty to carry out complete restoration at his own expense.

For all Beckett's idiosyncrasies, his basic viewpoint had cogency. A vocal and aesthetically not negligible school of thought at that period condemned church restoration of any kind – better to let them fall down, said one of its more extreme members – and much nineteenth-century work assuredly gives a certain excuse for their contention. As a sincerely practising Anglican Beckett wanted somewhere in which both he and later generations could worship, not a building that might collapse at almost any moment. At more worldly level he was also waging vehement war on the architectural profession, as represented by the Royal Institute of British Architects (of which he was for some years an honorary Associate), whom he accused, with much supporting evidence, of accepting high fees for misguided workmanship by men of eminent standing but dubious qualifications. He wanted a soundly built Abbey and no meddling inefficient architect; he himself knew about architecture and was a millionaire to boot. What simpler than that the job should be wholly in his hands? Both the Restoration Committee (or what was by that time left of it) and the town of St Albans were charmed to agree with him. Money talks. With such financial resources at his command their troubles were plainly at an end.

They were soon to be disillusioned. Exactly what they had hoped for is not clear to us even if it was to themselves – a conservative restoration sticking close to the original design, possibly, though with their previous knowledge of the man they should have known better. At any rate, Beckett had something very different in view – nor did the Abbey's elevation to Cathedral status change it. It may be that events played to some extent into his hands, parts of the fabric being found in worse condition than had been realised; whether they did or not is immaterial. His own designs for the Abbey-to-be raised an outcry both locally and in the non-professional as well as the architectural press; but Beckett was undeterred – the man who pays the piper calls the tune, was the gist of his reply. He knew very well what he was about. Filling *The Times*' correspondence columns with vituperative retorts to his detractors, he went inexorably ahead. Each new bit of restoration was greeted by protests. In the north transept his circular window, certainly looking like a diagram of ball-bearings in the hub of a wheel, exacerbated the outcry. His new west front in particular, still deplored by many, though surely no more mechanical and soulless than other church architecture of its time, was greeted with a howl of horror – but horror not without its lighter moments from those who enjoyed, as Beckett did not, a sense of humour:

The Church of Canterbury Town
Upon its head bears Beckett's crown,
St Albans to our wandering gaze
A Beckett's hinder end displays.

For some years the hullaballoo continued. That so pugnacious a man should make enemies was, of course, inevitable – indeed he might scarcely have been happy without them, particularly if they were architects. But there were some who, and not wholly without excuse, saw him in a more charitable light. After the opening of the restored nave in 1885 a luncheon at the *Peahen Hotel* was addressed by no less a person than the Bishop. 'Surely I am the most fortunate of bishops', declared his Lordship, 'for when my cathedral was tumbling down, a great layman came forward to build it up again. God bless him. God bless Sir Edmund Beckett for his good work towards this church.' On which Peter Ferriday comments: 'According-ing to one report on the luncheon the joke that went round the tables was that now Sir Edmund had done his good work the sooner he was called to his heavenly reward the better.'

By 1893 Beckett, by that time Lord Grimthorpe, had completed the job to his own satisfaction, if to few other people's, in the course of it going to law with another rich landowner over the restoration of the Lady Chapel. There stood the Abbey four-square upon its hill, its squat Norman tower good for another nine cen-turies, its turrets, windows, west front, Lady Chapel all gleaming in the sun. He also restored in similar enterprising fashion the churches of St Peter and St Michael. He died in 1905, aged 89. *Si monumentum requiris . . .* well, perhaps. It would be wrong to exaggerate the defects of his part in the Abbey today. A less con-troversial figure might have done worse and got away with it.

From the curious saga of St Albans Abbey – incidentally, the church with the longest nave in the world, some 300 feet long – my mind turns to a church in the extreme north of Hertfordshire, where the nave measures 33 feet by 14 feet and the chancel 17 feet by 14 feet. It serves a parish of less than 100 inhabitants – Caldecote a tiny backwater of a place, for all that the bustling A 1(M) is close at hand. Besides the church, there is only a farm with a couple of large barns and two or three cottages; least conspicuous of them all is the church, dedicated to St Mary Magdalene, so modest in size, so retiring between the barns and a clump of trees, so utterly peaceful, that to walk about it seems an affront and cold-bloodedly to analyse it, to anatomise it, an outrage. Of all churches in the county it is the one in which I, not a conventionally religious person, hear clearest the still small voice. Dating for the most part from the fourteenth century, it has a fine canopied stoup in the south porch, a fifteenth-century font and some fifteenth-century bench ends in the nave. But, as well as for the peace that envelopes me whenever I go there, I remember it also for old Mary Flint, the female parish clerk (against all canon law, I believe) who officiated in the early years of the last century and was buried in the churchyard in 1838, when she was 83. In the year of her death the *Church of England Magazine* so far acknowledged her existence as to publish a drawing of her – a wizened little woman in cloak and poke bonnet, gazing earnestly at the font in which her 19 children had been baptised.

Hertfordshire has a total of nearly 200 churches, of which more than half can rightly claim a visit, sometimes for their architectural qualities, sometimes for their human associations, sometimes, of course, for both. Into the last category falls that of Baldock, only a few miles from Caldecote, handsomely embattled, mostly of the fourteenth and fifteenth centuries but with earlier traces, its tower surmounted by an octagonal drum and 'spike' similar to that at Ashwell, which we shall visit next. Of its several brasses the most curious is that to Edmund Pym, rector of the neighbouring small parish of Radwell, who died in 1807; it is in fact the brass of an early fifteenth century woman cut off a little below the knees and furnished with an inscription, also in brass, to Pym. Elsewhere in the church are a good many slabs to the Goodwyns, Fitzjohns and Pryors, all prominent malting families in a town that for centuries lived largely by malting. An early nineteenth-century rector, by the way, was John Smith; when an undergraduate at Cambridge he was the first to decipher and transcribe the shorthand of Pepys' Diary – he is said to have ruined his eyesight over it. In 1825 his transcription was used in Lord Braybrooke's edition, the first to bring the diary to popular notice; the man to whom the edition owed its very existence received no more than a patronising mention in the noble editor's Preface.

Printed guides, full or slight, to many Hertfordshire churches and typewritten notes available for use in others, release me from the obligation to detail every one; but Ashwell, half a dozen miles by road north east of Baldock, defies omission.

Ashwell is a large, fascinating but nowadays sophisticated village, containing (in spite of a disastrous fire in 1850) such ancient buildings as the fourteenth-century Chantry House, the fifteenth-century Guildhouse, the Town House (now a local museum), several medieval farmhouses and the Merchant Taylors School of 1681, down to the Bury remodelled by Sir Edwin Lutyens in the 1920s. A small borough at the time of Domesday Book, it remained prosperous as a market and malting centre throughout the Middle Ages and beyond; was its inaccessible situation compared with either Baldock or Royston, both thoroughfare towns, responsible in part for its later decline? But it is of prosperity that the large church of St Mary, with a tower 176 feet in height, seems to speak.

Yet most of it was built in the half century following the Black Death of 1348 and 1349, though the two-storeyed south porch and the timber lychgate at the entrance to the churchyard are somewhat later. The interior, with for the most part clear glass windows, is disappointingly bare of monuments and brasses; it owes its exceptional interest to medieval doodling, or something rather like it – to the *graffiti* on the walls of the tower and columns of the nave. Here in Latin we may read of the 'miserable, wild, distracted dregs of a people' who survived the slaughter of the Black Death and of the five-day tempest that 'thundered in the world' on the feast of St Maurus (15 January) in 1361, probably about the time at which building operations were beginning. There is also a bold and admirably executed representation of a church, often said to be either Westminster Abbey (to whom the manor of Ashwell belonged) or old St Paul's Cathedral but more likely the composite dream of a medieval architect. Also on the walls of the tower is a builder's wage sheet and check-list of materials; and too an inscription of which all that can be deciphered is '. . . *cana sit libera*', the opening phrase of Magna Carta, 'Let the English Church be free'.

It has always seemed to me dangerous trustfulness that leaves these remarkable *graffiti* entirely unprotected; warnings there are in the surrounding – and, I think, encroaching – deeply scratched initials of eighteenth- and nineteenth-century sightseers. Safer, because often difficult to detect, are the small Latin inscriptions on the nave columns – 'The corners are not pointed correctly – I spit at them', 'Drunkenness breaks whatever wisdom touches', 'The girl Barbara is a barbarian' and others.

A few miles east of Ashwell, Royston church, dedicated to St John and St Thomas and part of an Augustinian Priory founded in the twelfth century, was so heavily restored in 1872 that it is now of only minor architectural interest; but it contains the slabs of two of Royston's oldest families, the Worthams and the Beldams, as well as the tomb of Henry Andrews (died 1820) who 'from a limited education' rose to be employed as mathematician by the Commissioners of the Board of Longitude and also to make for its proprietors all the mathematical and astrological calculations for *Old Moore's Almanack*. Elsewhere in the neighbourhood, Reed shows Saxon long-and-short work in its tower and a good early Norman doorway; Therfield rectory dates in part from the fifteenth century; Barley has a Norman tower and Barkway contains a monument to Admiral Sir John Jennings (died 1743) by Rysbrack. Not far from Barkway the little church of Anstey is unusual in having escaped almost all restoration; the lower stages of the tower are late Norman, most of the rest of the fabric about a century later. There is also a Norman font; and in the churchyard part of the lychgate has been turned into a parish lock-up.

From Anstey a south-westerly cross-country run through Wyddial brings us to Buntingford, one of the places which, as I mentioned in a previous chapter, has moved its site from hilltop to high road. On the hilltop of Layston stands the old church of St Bartholomew, mostly fifteenth-century but with earlier fragments. At what date it finally went out of use I do not know – I fancy that occasional services were held until relatively recent years. Then followed a period of neglect; but very soon after the Second World War it was patched up, its nave unroofed and the chancel used as a chapel for the modern burial ground close by. Meanwhile Buntingford folk normally continued to attend the chapel (now the parish church) of St Peter at the south end of the village, built about 1612, restored in 1899 and containing a brass to its builder, Alexander Strange, showing him in the pulpit before his congregation and with an hourglass at hand.

If my readers choose to extend this detour through rather charming scenery, they may visit Cottered, where St John's has a well-preserved wall painting of St Christopher, and Ardeley, where a Victorian lord of the manor, incensed at the vicar's proposal to do away with the squire's pew, threw hymn-books at him in the pulpit during a Sunday morning service.

And now back through Buntingford and Hare Street to our former southward route.

In the three Pelhams the most interesting church is that of Furneux (pronounced Furnix) Pelham, surrounded by what until relatively recent years was a circular churchyard. It is a large and rather handsome building for so small a village, a good deal restored but containing several interesting tombs, brasses (including a fine one to a civilian and his wife, about 1428), a window with glass by William Morris and another by Morris and Burne Jones. Its curiosity, however, is the inscription on the clock of the tower, 'Time Flies. Mind your Business'. It is said that the clock, with its original inscription, came in the early seventeenth century from the nearby Furneux Pelham Hall; a minute hand was added rather more than a century ago. But on a repainting of the inscription in 1906 the word 'own' between 'your' and 'business' was, perhaps from motives of tact, omitted.

By way of Braughing (pronounced Braffing), whose fifteenth-century church is as picturesquely set in the midst of its village as any in east Hertfordshire, it is not difficult to reach Standon, in the Middle Ages a borough and still a most attractive spot, with a wide High Street flanked by houses of many periods. Here the church of

St Mary is unique in the county for two reasons – its detached tower and, through being built into a hillside, its three levels: from the large west porch steps lead to the nave and more steps from nave to chancel. The nave, by the way, was mostly rebuilt about 1865. Its two most conspicuous monuments – and fine they are – recall Sir Ralph Sadleir, builder of Standon Lordship, who died in 1587, and his son, Sir Thomas (died 1606); alongside the former are hung his helmet, sword, spurs and standard pole. Sir Thomas, with his wife by his side, was one of the keepers of Mary, Queen of Scots, in her captivity. There are two equally fine brasses, the best being to John Field, merchant of the Staple of Calais, and his son (1474). What I have failed to find, however, is any memorial to Richard Goff or Gaff (though the parish registers record his burial), who in 1805 at the age of 87 married a woman aged 30, having already had two children by her; three more were born to them, in 1805, 1807 and 1815. Goff died in 1819, aged 101. Nor, to retrace my steps for a moment, have I discovered 'in the church room' at Braughing the tablet to a vicar, unveiled in 1904, which, according to a notebook kept by a long succession of incumbents, was the work of 'Mr A. E. R. Gill' – that is, the young Eric Gill (1882-1940), later well known as sculptor of the figure of Ariel over the main entrance to Broadcasting House in London and also as the designer of a distinguished typeface.

In part a Roman road, A 120 leads to Little Hadham, whose church is one of only four in England dedicated to St Cecilia, patroness of music; southward lies the far more opulent Much Hadham, for centuries owned by the Bishops of London and whose church, St Andrew's, alongside their palace is worthy of such a distinction. It embraces all styles between the thirteenth and fifteenth centuries – a building of great dignity and considerable richness of detail; see, for instance, the splendid roofing of both the nave and chancel and the beautifully sculptured heads of some of the nave capitals and corbels – grotesque animals, a couple of clowns, a portrait said to be of Edward III and one of a bishop, said to be Bishop Courtney, before whom Wycliffe was brought in 1377. There are also traces of wall painting and some fifteenth-century stained glass – though more was taken during restoration in 1845 by a contractor who claimed it as part of his perquisites. Its brasses too are notable – to a rector, Simon Lambard (1332), to another rector, Alban (1372), to a third priest, in academic dress (1420), as well as several later ones, including those to Clement Newce and his wife (late sixteenth century) and their 19 children and to William Newce, his wife and 13 children. A sixteenth-century rector, Alexander Nowell, it may be added, is credited by Izaak Walton with the discovery of bottled beer – an ardent fisherman, he accidentally left his beer, contained in a leather bottle, in the grass, returning some days later to find it greatly improved and with a splendid head on it.

To say that the chief point of interest in the great church of St Michael at Bishop's Stortford, with a 182-foot tower and spire, is its dominating position above the town may sound disparaging; but it is in fact one of the few Hertfordshire churches to impose itself upon the view, most of them merging inconspicuously into the immediate landscape. The upper stages of the tower were rebuilt between 1810 and 1820; cut into the stringcourse just below the battlements is the inscription: 'This tower was built by parish expense but a mean parish that gave the workmen nothing to drink.' Its clock was the work of John Briant of Hertford, the late eighteenth- and early nineteenth-century caster of many Hertfordshire bells; it has a pendulum 18 feet long, the longest for miles around. Most of the church is Perpendicular in style, with a typical east window; it has fine roofs, though the whole building underwent restoration by Sir Arthur Blomfield in 1869. The pulpit is, rather surprisingly, of the Commonwealth period, 1658, and there is a handsome fifteenth-century rood screen – part of the beam that formerly carried the rood now embellishes the *Boar's Head* close by. The chancel stalls, said to have come from old St Paul's Cathedral, have poppy heads and grotesquely carved misericords, while the corbels of the nave show not only figures of the Apostles but also, among others, a gardener with a pruning knife, a cook with a ladle, a woodman with a billhook – and a man with a stomach ache. Apart from Richard Fletcher, whom the antiquary, Camden, reports as 'dying from the immoderate use of tobacco', Bishop Stortford's best-known vicar was Francis William Rhodes, father of Cecil Rhodes; his vicarage in South Street is now a Rhodes museum.

A few miles down A 11 Sawbridgeworth is to be visited, if for nothing else, for its brasses – several, one of them a grand specimen, to the Leventhorpes of Shingle Hall (a medieval manor) and three to the Chauncys of Pishiobury. It is unfortunate, however, that in 1968 thieves gravely damaged the brass to Joan Leventhorpe, 1527 (who had already lost that of her husband many years ago), in trying to prise it from its indent; it is now in safe keeping in the vestry chest. Incidentally, the same gang had better luck at Great Amwell in carrying off a unique brass, about 1440, to a friar; and at the same time the brass to Sir Rowland Lytton of Knebworth was damaged. There are also at Sawbridgeworth rich sixteenth-, seventeenth- and eighteenth-century monuments to local dignitaries.

Stanstead Abbots on A 414 has two churches – one, built in 1880 and by good luck almost covered in greenery; the other, St James's, Early English, Perpendicular and with a fine fifteenth-century porch, is without a doubt a gem unchanged since the eighteenth century, with whitewashed walls, box pews, three-decker pulpit, royal coat of arms, hatchments, some small brasses, a sixteenth-century tomb and so on – all typical of a hundred Rowlandson prints. Its wonderful eighteenth-century character is only slightly modified by memorials to three nineteenth-century members of the Booth family, the distillers. But since services are seldom held here it is unfortunately (or should I say, fortunately?) kept locked and the casual visitor, unless he is lucky, must content himself with gazing through its windows. That, I insist, is something he must not miss – and, of course, the building's charming setting, with a deep-hedged lane and the lush Lea valley on one side and an extremely picturesque Stanstead Bury on the other. The noisy main road only a few yards off is the intrusion of a barbarian world.

Two or three miles away, Ware has, I repeat from a previous chapter, become in the last quarter of a century one of Hertfordshire's most ravaged towns; but its church, St Mary's, has survived pretty drastic restoration in 1848, 1885, and 1905 to remain even today the natural focus of an ancient centre both of agriculture and

of industry. It is a handsome structure, relatively unusual in having
transepts; its pride is an octagonal font of about 1400, with figures
of the Virgin, Saints and angels – 'the most richly carved font in
the county', says Pevsner. A good many of its old tombs have been
removed; but we may justly remember it as the burial place of the
Fanshawe family, sixteenth- and seventeenth-century lords of the
manor, the most notable of whom was Sir Richard, diplomatist,
Ambassador and poet, husband of the Lady Anne whose Memoirs
describe most movingly the privations and dangers she shared with
him during the Civil War and the niggardly reward for loyalty
granted by Charles II. In the churchyard is the tomb-chest of William
Meade, who died in 1652, aged (according to the inscription) 148
years 9 months 7 weeks and 5 days – 'perhaps', suggested the
humorous county historian, Cussans, 'the explanation of this extra-
ordinary instance of longevity may lie in the fact that the doctor was
a vendor of Life Pills and that the tombstone was erected by a successor to his practice'. Though never claiming an equal life-span,
Ware has had some interesting vicars, including Charles Chauncy,
who became second President of Harvard; one of its eighteenth-
century curates, John Trusler, conceived the ingenious (and, as it
turned out, profitable) scheme of printing in manuscript 150 sermons
to be bought by parsons unwilling to write their own. A noncon-
formist minister here was Charles Lamb's friend, the revolutionary
William Godwin; and an usher in a Ware school, Alexander Cruden,
compiled the famous Concordance.

Before taking a different direction it may be noted that the only
place of worship in Hertford that is of much interest is the Friends'
Meeting House, erected in 1670 and most tactfully restored in 1953
the oldest meeting house built for Quakers that is still in use.

It is strange that a countryside so rapidly falling prey to modern
isation of all kinds should contain, at no great distance from each
other, two churches whose great charm lies in their complete
remoteness from the modern world – St James at Stanstead Abbot
and little St John the Baptist at Great Amwell. The latter, perched
above the romantically landscaped spring that was one of the original
sources of the New River, is an oasis of blessed silence – almost

entirely Norman, with an apsidal chancel (similar to one at St Leonard's, Bengeo, north of Hertford) and small fifteenth-century tower. Outside its south porch is a scratch dial; in its churchyard are stocks and, among other monuments, the large mausoleum of the Mylne family, one of them designer and builder of the first Black-friars Bridge over the Thames and for two generations engineers and architects to the New River Company. A seventeenth-century vicar, Thomas Hassall, by the way, most fortunately for historians and others allowed garrulity ample scope in his parish registers; though he records disasters and pestilence ('God in his mercy turn this and all other his plagues from us') he is not above occasional solemn skittishness in recording baptisms – as, for instance, in 1633:

> Amye, the abortive daughter of Bridget Newman betrothed to one ffrancis Todde who should have bin married on Michael-masse daye untimely borne the daye before so turninge the mariage feast into a christeninge.

Hoddesdon's church of St Paul, burial place in 1869 of Harriet Auber, who wrote 'Our blest Redeemer ere He breathed', was built in 1732 (but largely rebuilt in the succeeding century) because the lord of the manor quarrelled with the vicar of Broxbourne, of which parish Hoddesdon was then a hamlet. In Broxbourne itself St Augustine's is delightfully situated on a bluff above the Lea and facing a large greensward that is lined by very respectable Victorian houses, relics of the immediate post-railway development of the 1840s. Mostly Perpendicular but with a Decorated west window, St Augustine's has, however, a south porch of about 1650; the handsome Saye chapel was built in 1522. The size and richness of the whole structure underlines the importance of the great road to York that ran close by many centuries before the railway was thought of. In it are the tombs of Sir John Saye (1474), Sir William Saye and other notables, some, judging by their inscriptions, of exceptional virtue; and also of Edward Christian (1829), brother of Fletcher who was leader of the *Bounty* mutineers. A tablet commemorates John Loudon McAdam, 'the great Improver of the British Roads', who spent the last years of his life in the house now occupied by Lloyd's Bank. There are also some interesting fifteenth- and sixteenth-century brasses.

But frankly, two personalities connected with Broxbourne church intrigue me quite as much as the building. One was Francis Thackeray, uncle of the novelist, curate for nine years and buried here in 1842 – another (but, I believe, unconnected) ecclesiastical Thackeray in the opening years of this century, by the way, raised a local storm by obtaining the licence of a public house and conducting services from behind the bar. The other intriguing personality, William Jones, for 20 years curate and for 20 vicar, died in 1821, having for the great part of his days kept a diary recording not only a multitude of Broxbourne happenings of all kinds but also the ups and downs of his married life. A separate Book of Domestic Lamentations, to which he more than once refers, has, however, been lost; though in later years he and his wife came into loving concord and are buried side by side, one wonders whether its loss may not be due to her having outlived him.

St Mary's at Cheshunt, soon to have its peace disturbed by road changes, need not detain us long, except to note that the rector who built it between 1418 and 1448, Nicholas Dixon, was also a Baron of the Exchequer. It contains, amongst others, the tomb of Henry Atkins, physician to James 1 and Charles 1, both of whom owned the nearby mansion of Theobalds. In the immediate neighbourhood, Cheshunt college was established by Selina, the late eighteenth-century Countess of Huntingdon, to train ministers for her break-away sect of the Wesleyans; it now, however, belongs to the Church of England.

So far we have travelled steady southwards; we must now turn west, where more churches claim attention, though few close attention. At Northaw, for instance, St Thomas the Martyr, dating from 1882, is the third on the site; its immediate predecessor was built in the early nineteenth century in order, it is said, to enable the squire to worship in his own pew, well removed from the common people. Potters Bar offers us nothing. But St Mary's at North Mymms is a rather different matter.

Well retired from the noisy Barnet by-pass, A 1, largely surrounded by trees and close to its seventeenth-century vicarage, it is a pleasant fourteenth-century structure apparently intended to have a central tower in place of its present west one of rather later date – and transepts too, perhaps, though these, like the tower, were never built. Much of its furnishing, including the pulpit, is Elizabethan. Its principal tomb is the large one of John, Lord Somers of Brookmans, whom I mentioned in my chapter on houses – a tomb which did not wholly please our old friend, Cussans: 'On the edge of a sarcophagus of black marble is seated, in a most uncomfortable position, a large figure of Justice, fat and scantily draped.' Elsewhere are tombs of the Conyngsbys of North Mymms Park and others. It contains also some notable brasses, particularly a fine Flemish one to William de Kestevene (1361) and also to a fifteenth-century Elizabeth Knollys, whose husband, an effigy in armour, has been lost. Thirdly, with an unusually long inscription, a brass to Richard Butler and his wife, he in Elizabethan armour.

At South Mimms (note the different spelling of the place name) the church of St Giles has a thirteenth-century chancel, a fourteenth-century nave and a fifteenth-century tower; but its interior was swept fairly clean by G. E. Street in 1877. He had, however, the grace to leave a fine sixteenth-century oak screen separating the Frowyke chapel from the rest of the building, as well as some Frowyke tombs and brasses. The Frowykes were lords of a local manor for two or more centuries. There is also in the church some good sixteenth-century glass. It may be added that until 1896 this large parish embraced not only Potters Bar but also nearly all one side of Barnet High Street.

Pretty nearly a clean sweep was made too of St Botolph's, Shenley, during a restoration as early as 1753. But not quite all has been lost there; it still contains, besides some poppy head bench ends and the original sanctuary ring on an oak door, the tomb of Nicholas Hawksmoor (died 1736), assistant to Wren in the building of Greenwich Hospital, to Vanburgh at Castle Howard and Blenheim, and independent architect of several London churches as well as the towers of Westminster Abbey. The rectory, by the way, was occupied by the Newcombe family from 1742 to 1905 – a span of 163 years – with the exception of five years between 1797 and 1802.

To continue quoting Cussans, if perhaps to be reprehended, is quite irresistible – especially at Aldenham, the tower of whose fine church, St John's, was damaged by bombs in the Second World War. It contains a wealth of memorials – though Cussans tells of a nineteenth-century baker in Watford who lined his oven with stones from the churchyard. 'If his customers wanted a loaf well baked they would order one with Sacred to the Memory on the bottom of it . . . if on the contrary they preferred it slack-baked they would insist on having *Requiescat in Pace*.' And written in to his personal copy of his History, now in the County Record Office (which contains many stories that he considered, and quite rightly, unprintable in his own day) he enlarges upon a tablet – still on the walls, I think – erected in 1864 by Judith and Elizabeth Gee to the memory of their parents. Added to it is the name of Judith, the wife of Thomas Gee of Wadhurst, Sussex, who died in 1875.

> Thomas Gee of Wadhurst, Esquire, is still (in 1883) living, but in Aldenham is commonly known as Tom Castle. He was for many years a butler in the Gee family. One day after the death of Mrs Gee he came into the Drawing Room where Judith and Elizabeth were together and said he intended leaving. They were astonished and asked him if he were dissatisfied with his wages. 'No', he said, 'hit hisn't that Hi'm not content with my sellery, but hif you want me to stop Hi must marry one o' you two ladies hand Hi don't care which.' In order to retain the services of so excellent a man as Tom Castle the two virgins – both upwards of 40 – cast lots which should offer herself on the hymeneal alter. The lot was Judy's and Tom Castle, butler blossomed into Thomas Gee Esquire. N.B. There are no little Gees.

Collins' *Guide to English Parish Churches*, edited by Sir John Betjeman, describes the church of St Mary at Watford as 'an oasis of quiet in Hertfordshire's largest, ugliest and noisiest town'. So long a

Hertfordshire alone is in question the smear on Watford may in part be true; on the other hand, there are plenty of uglier towns all over the country. But that the church is an oasis of quiet is undeniable. It lies in its churchyard just off the admittedly noisy High Street and south of the old market-place, its massive tower, once a landmark, now glimpsed for the most part between large modern shops and offices. It has, however, been discreetly restored and retains much restful dignity – a pleasant refuge from a mad world. The chancel is mostly of the thirteenth century, the nave and tower of the fifteenth, while the Morrison, or Essex, chapel was built in 1595 by Bridget, Countess of Bedford, widow of Sir Richard Morrison. This contains the splendid tombs of many of the Morrison family, owners of the now demolished mansion of Cassiobury, on the outskirts of the town, before it was acquired by the Capels, Earls of Essex, who also lie here. Elsewhere in the church, among a host of fascinating memorials of all kinds, is a tablet to Jane Bell (1773), with inscription by Dr Johnson.

In the churchyard is the eighteenth-century tomb-chest, enclosed by an iron railing, of Benjamin Wangford, out of which grows a tree – a similar phenomenon can be seen at Aldenham and Tewin. In all cases legend has it that the deceased denied the doctrine of immortality; the living tree springing from a dead body gave, it is claimed, the lie to such blasphemy. There is too the vault of the eighteenth- and nineteenth-century Clutterbuck family, influential brewers (with brewery at Edgware, Middlesex) and large landowners in west Hertfordshire. One of them, Robert, compiled a *History of Hertfordshire*, published between 1815 and 1830, a most valuable record but much the driest reading of any of the county's four, though a fifth, this century's *Victoria County History*, runs it close. Almost adjoining the churchyard, by the way, stands Mrs Elizabeth Fuller's Free School, built in 1704, functioning until the 1880s and now used for parish purposes.

We can very nearly bypass Bushey and Rickmansworth – except for an unusual tympanum of royal arms (Queen Anne) and a seventeenth-century pulpit at the former and at the latter a part-medieval vicarage containing French sixteenth-century glass from the church before restoration – and plunge into rich Chiltern country on the borders of Hertfordshire and Buckinghamshire.

The church of the Holy Cross at Sarratt is unusual in having a saddle-back roof to its tower – that is, the ridge line of the roof is at right angles to that of the chancel and nave. Parts of the building are Norman, but the whole underwent a good deal of restoration by Sir George Gilbert Scott in 1865 – incidentally, under a rector who was in charge of the parish from 1859 to 1912. Scott also built the present church of St Mary Magdelene at Flaunden in 1838 – his first job, he says in his Memoirs. It contains the font from the old church, which went out of use when the new was built and is now nothing but a few crumbling walls in the form of a Greek cross. During the latter part of last century and even then in a woefully dilapidated condition, it became a poor farmhouse; the story goes that the farmer's wife used to sit broody hens in the font, not yet transferred to the new building.

With King's Langley we re-enter the diesel- and petrol-fumed civilisation of A 41. In my chapter on castles I dealt at some length with this extremely interesting place: suffice it to say here that All Saints', dating principally from the fifteenth century, contains the elaborately heraldic tomb of Edmund of Langley, fifth son of Edward III, and a couple of good palimpsest brasses, as well as a Westmacott epitaph to Mary Elizabeth Crawford, who died in 1793.

Only two or three miles further on, Hemel Hempstead – incontestably the most attractive of Hertfordshire's New Towns – can also boast one of Hertfordshire's finest churches. Though large, it is not unduly so – Hitchin, for instance, is rather larger; what gives it special value is the fact that it is almost uniformly Norman in style, though Perpendicular windows have nearly everywhere been substituted for the older ones. Moreover the chancel and the narrow chamber on the north side of it are rib-vaulted and there is a Norman clerestory – both genuine rarities. It is in two senses further conspicuous for its lead-covered spire, first erected in 1689, rising nearly 200 feet above the town – one of the very few of Hertfordshire's old churches to be spired. Though in later centuries Hemel Hempstead achieved a genuine regional importance, in the twelfth, when the church was built, it was no more than a small and struggling market town like many another, not even lying on the great thoroughfare (now A 41) to London. Domesday Book, however, shows its territory to have been divided between a Norman baron and St Albans Abbey; was it under Abbey auspices that so ambitious a church was planned?

But if the fabric itself is something on no account to be missed, the same cannot, alas, be said for its interior decoration by G. F. Bodley in 1885. Still, passing that over, the same interior, besides a handsome late fifteenth-century brass to Robert Albyn and his wife, contains many intriguing memorials of local interest – including a large wall tablet to Sir Astley Paston Cooper, 'of the ancient family of Paston in the County of Norfolk', who died in 1841, having been surgeon to George IV, William IV and Victoria – and also a formidable opponent of the London and Birmingham railway, which from 1838 ran alongside his park at Gadebridge. On the same tablet his wife, who died in 1827, is described as 'pious without enthusiasm' – a curious survival of that eighteenth-century epithet to indicate unobtrusive piety, 'enthusiasm' being commonly employed to denigrate the more exuberant followers of John Wesley.

A little further along our road is St Peter's at Berkhamsted, a massive building of the thirteenth, fourteenth and fifteenth centuries, restored by Sir Jeffry Wyattville in 1820 (who covered the exterior with stucco), again by William Butterfield in 1870 (who refaced it in flint) and a third time in 1960. Various points are to be noted here – firstly, that nave and chancel are out of alignment; secondly, that the nave pillars bear slightly outwards; thirdly, that the two west bays of the south aisle are windowless – against them once stood a structure occupied at different times by Royalist prisoners and the parish fire engine. Near the south transept, St John's Chantry Chapel was for three and a half centuries used exclusively by the boys and masters of Berkhamsted School – once in the early eighteenth century the ceiling fell in, luckily just when the boys 'were all gone into the body of the church to attend the catechising'. Note also in the gallery the royal arms of Elizabeth I, under which is written:

This mighty Queen is dead, and lives,
And leaves the world to wonder,
How she a maiden Queen did rule,
Few Kings have gone beyond her.

Among the church's wealth of memorials may I select four for attention – a brass to John Raven (1385), who served with the Black Prince; a brass inscription, 1509, to Robert Incent, father of the John who founded Berkhamsted School; and the mutilated tomb of Robert Baldwin, who died in 1639 bequeathing his share in 'waterworks' in Hyde Park to the Berkhamsted poor – waterworks afterwards submerged in the creation of the Serpentine. Finally the large east window, installed in 1872, commemorates William Cowper, the poet, born in 1731 at the rectory (demolished a century and a half ago) in which lived his father, the rector, nephew of the first Earl Cowper of Cole Green near Hertford. When the shy little lad was only six his mother, the apple of his eye, died suddenly; whereupon his father, well intentioned but tragically mistaken, set him on the course of schooling at Markyate Street that led later to Dr Nathanial Cotton's Collegium Insanorum in St Albans and finally to the enforced quietude of Olney.

Berkhamsted is, however, only a later settlement of what is now the separate parish of Northchurch, where St Mary's is of Saxon origin, though no Saxon work is visible except to the expert eye. In addition to a wall tablet to Matthew Brook, who was a bellringer here from 1844 to 1915, its most interesting memorial is a late eighteenth-century brass (scorned by serious brass enthusiasts) to Peter the Wild Boy, an idiot incapable of speech or learning, found in a German forest, brought to England by Queen Caroline, exhibited for a time at Court, farmed out at an allowance of £35 a year to a Northchurch farmer and, after various adventures, dying in 1785 at the supposed age of 75, to be buried at Government expense.

In spite of its picturesque setting, St Peter and St Paul's at Tring must detain us only long enough to examine the intriguing figures of men and animals carved in the spandrels of the nave arcades and the bays of the clerestory; and also the pompous monument, probably by Grinling Gibbons, of Sir William Gore (died 1707) of Tring Park – Sir William's thumb, by the way, lost for more than a century, was rescued from a pond in 1881 and restored to its rightful place. The Tring parish registers, it is interesting to add, record the burial of the great-great-grandmother of George Washington and the baptism of her son, though not the son from whom George was descended.

Nor, alas, must we stay at the church of St John the Baptist at Aldbury, except to note its fine Perpendicular stone screen, the monument of Sir Robert Whittingham (1471), the notable fifteenth-century brass to Sir Ralph Verney and his wife – and also the old mahogany pitch-pipe, on which, in pre-organ or church orchestra days, the clerk gave the note for singing. Equally we must hurry by the church of St John the Baptist at Great Gaddesden, with, amongst others, a monument to Agatha Halsey (1782) by Flaxman and the church of St Peter and St Paul at Little Gaddesden, with a wealth of monuments (and revoltingly fulsome inscriptions) to the Bridgewater family of Ashridge – and on to Redbourn, where St Mary's is largely Norman, with Roman bricks in the walls of its tower, probably slightly earlier in date than Hemel Hempstead. It has a noteworthy fifteenth-century rood screen and parts of the delicately traceried rood loft. And thus through Harpenden to Wheathampstead, until 1859 both forming a united parish of over 10,000 acres and less than 5,000 parishioners.

It was mid-nineteenth century restoration that gave us St Mary's curious spire which, as Pevsner points out, starts like a pyramidal roof and finishes like the point of a pencil. In the Middle Ages Wheathampstead belonged to Westminster Abbey; does the size and fine quality of this mere parish church reflect a desire on Westminster's part to keep more or less topsides with the splendour of St Alban's Abbey a few miles away? The thought, though probably fantastic, is perhaps teasing; certainly the two Abbeys were for centuries at daggers drawn, even coming several times to blows over rival claims to No Man's Land Common lying between their respective territories. The interior of St Mary's, however, is largely given over to the post-medieval tombs and memorials of the Garrard family of Lamer Park, whose fine old house is now demolished. The first Garrard came to Lamer in 1555, the last left it in 1948. He was Apsley Cherry Garrard, author of *The Worst Journey in the World*, one of the classics of Arctic exploration.

Only by a cross-country journey along narrow winding lanes, very charming in themselves, can we reach Hitchin, our next important port of call. On the way it is worth stopping at Whitwell (the parish is St Paul's Walden) to see the incongruous but in itself handsome eighteenth-century chancel (with remarkable chancel arch) of the church of All Saints. Close by, St Paul's Waldenbury has been held for two centuries by ancestors of the present Queen; and 100 years ago, even with no royal connection in prospect, there was no doubt about their status. Lady Glamis (who died in the 1880s) used, it is said, to arrive at the church on Sunday mornings attended by a large retinue of servants and followed by a page-boy carrying a prayerbook wrapped in a silk handkerchief. When at her leisure she and all her staff had settled themselves in their various pews – and only then – the clerk would tap gently on the vestry door and murmur to the vicar within, 'Time, sir'.

Quite near St Paul's Walden is King's Walden, where St Mary's has a south window by William Morris. 'How noble and susceptible to the nature of the glass-painter's material', says Pevsner, 'does such a window appear, if one compares it with other Victorian stained glass.'

We may also call in passing at Offley, where St Mary's, in addition to an early nineteenth-century brick tower, has like St Paul's Walden, an eighteenth-century chancel. This one was built by Sir Robert Salusbury, uncle of Dr Johnson's Mrs Thrale; the pretentious monument to Sir Robert and his wife is by Nollekens. The well-known medieval historian, G. G. Coulton, who was a curate at Offley in the 1880s, tells in his recollections, *Fourscore Years*, how, in the absence of the vicar on holiday, he had to collect attendance fees from the village school. Some time after the vicar's return he handed the money over. To his surprise it was received with evident embarrassment – which was by no means lessened when the vicar's wife innocently exclaimed, 'Why Alfred – and you've balanced the school accounts without it!'

Of all Hertfordshire churches, St Mary's at Hitchin, in a spacious churchyard partly enclosed by two-storeyed period houses, nearly all of them discreetly converted into shops, in part open to the canalised and landscaped Hiz and the large modern market place and bus station beyond it, is by far the most handsomely displayed – indeed, the visitor arriving by bus or coach and being greeted by so immensely rewarding a view might excusably entertain high hopes for the rest of the town. Alas, during the last 20 or so years Hitchin has diligently sloughed off almost all its historic and aesthetic merit – not with the semi-plausible excuse of Ware, Hertfordshire's other ravaged town, that it was being overwhelmed by heavy traffic but in order to substitute the mediocrity of petty trading. St Mary's remains, thank God, inviolate. Rather more than 170 feet in total length and embattled throughout, it dates from the twelfth century, as seen to some extent in the buttresses of the tower, to the fifteenth of the fine Perpendicular east window. Its most notable portion, however, is the two-storeyed south porch, with elaborate lierne vaulting and bearing the arms of the Staple of Calais – Hitchin was a busy medieval wool town – the figures in its niches traditionally said to have been destroyed by Cromwellian soldiery. Inside the church, the roofs are all of fine craftsmanship – and notice also the grand series of oak screens beautifully traceried. Everywhere, in short, the woodwork is of the highest order. Its monuments and brasses are of all periods from the medieval, through the seventeenth- and eighteenth-century Radcliffes of Hitchin Priory, to Robert Hinde, died 1786, said to be the original of Sterne's Uncle Toby. Living at Preston, three or four miles away, he maintained an 'army' of farm hands and children, whom he used to parade round Hitchin to drum and trumpet in celebration of some battle or other event, retiring to Preston to fire a salute of guns from his formidably drawbridged house.

Through Great Wymondley, whose St Mary's has a Norman apsidal chancel like those at Great Amwell and Bengeo, to Stevenage, with another rare Hertfordshire spire to the church of St Nicholas nearly a mile from the middle of the old town. The tower itself is Norman, the rest of the building in various later styles. It contains a brass to Stephen Hallard (1506) and some interesting memorials – one, for instance, to Charlotte Amelia Hinde Whittington, 'the last member of her much respected family' and a well authenticated descendant of the famous Dick. Another is to Sara, 'late wife of Richard Bowcocke of the *Swan* in this town', who 'had two daughters, one abortive the other named Sara' and who died in 1660, aged 32. Bowcocke will be remembered by readers of Pepys as 'the best host I know of almost'; the *Swan*, no longer an inn, still stands opposite the fork of the Great North Road and the road (A 602) to Hitchin.

A couple of miles or so to the south, at Knebworth, are two churches worth attention. One, St Martin's, on the Great North Road, is by Sir Edwin Lutyens, built, like his Golf Clubhouse at the north end of the place, in the 1920s. The other, St Mary and St Thomas, lies a long way off, near the old village and Knebworth House, from which it is separated by a screen of trees planted in the opening years of the nineteenth century by Elizabeth Barbara Bulwer Lytton, mother of the novelist, following a quarrel with the rector over the legality of tithe paid on pineapples grown under glass. In addition she forbade all her house and estate staff to worship there, reading service herself in her own drawing room, and, rather than seem to have capitulated, was buried not in the churchyard but in a mausoleum in her own grounds. The church is nevertheless full of Lytton memorials.

Passing through Woolmer Green, where the furnishings of St Michael's (built in 1900) are by Ernest Gimson, at Welwyn the church of St Mary has a tablet to Dr Edward Young, the rector who died in 1765; his lengthy poem, usually known by the short title of *Night Thoughts* and including the line 'Procrastination is the thief of time', achieved in its day enormous popularity, was translated into almost every known language but is now completely forgotten. From Welwyn, however, it is convenient to visit Datchworth, where an inn owned by the parish once stood conveniently in the churchyard, Digswell, with perhaps the finest brass in the county – that to John Perient (1415) – and the Ayots. St Peter's at Ayot St Peter contains ceramic work by the four Martin Brothers, executed in about 1880; at Ayot St Lawrence the two churches, both dedicated to that saint, are the subject of a curious story. Briefly, the old church was still in use when in the late 1780s the lord of the manor, Sir Lionel Lyde, set about building a new house for himself. Conceiving that the church, admittedly in bad repair, disturbed the view from his windows, he began forthwith to demolish it. The Bishop of Lincoln (in whose diocese the parish then stood) protested; but on Sir Lionel's promise to build another appears to have been mollified. Hence the classical eyecatcher by Nicholas Revett, consecrated by the Bishop in 1799. The consecration at an end, said the *Gentleman's Magazine*, they 'all returned to the Mansion House [Sir Lionel's new house] where an elegant dinner was provided, after which the company dispersed for various innocent rural games until the close of the day and at last parted highly delighted'.

In 1948 some newly erected wrought-iron gates at the entrance to the old churchyard gave at their formal opening occasion for Ayot's most famous resident, George Bernard Shaw, to make a (for him) surprising speech, which concluded, 'This is His house, this is His gate, and this is His way'.

We have already visited some notable parish churches in the county – Ashwell, Hemel Hempstead, Hitchin and others; the tally would not be complete without St Etheldreda's at Hatfield, dominating from its hilltop the old town below and even Hatfield House at its side. In the past it dominated more than that – until the nineteenth century the Great North Road ran only a few yards off, between it and the old Tudor palace, with the fine inn known as the *Salisbury Arms* (now a block of flats) just opposite and the market hall, now demolished, close at hand. It was the very heart of Hatfield. A good deal of restoration of the fabric took place in 1872, particularly in the 100-foot-long and very spacious nave; but much original work of remarkable quality remains – notably the fifteenth-century Brocket Chapel and the early sixteenth-century Salisbury Chapel, the latter entered by splendid eighteenth-century gates from Amiens cathedral. (The gates in the churchyard, by the way, are from St Paul's; they date from about 1710.) The oldest parts are

the thirteenth-century chancel and transepts and the massive
fifteenth-century tower. The south transept window is by William
Morris and Burne Jones, wonderfully glowing in its rich colours.

Collins' *Guide to English Parish Churches*, which I have quoted
before, refers to St Etheldreda's as built 'to the Glory of God and
the House of Cecil'. This is surely unfair. What is more natural
than that the Salisburys, living, so to speak, next door, should regard
it, like any other parishioners, as quite naturally their last resting
place? And would it not have been false modesty on their part to be
buried hugger-mugger in inconspicuous graves? The large monument
to Robert, first Earl, who died in 1612, shows him not only in full
ceremonial costume but also as a skeleton, as though, despite his
high standing, he was well aware of his ultimate status. Other
Salisbury tombs may be less frank in this respect – what they lack
in humility they recover in pomp; but they are certainly no more
ostentatious than those of lesser men elsewhere. That of the third
Marquess, three times Prime Minister, who was buried here in 1903,
has its replica in Westminster Abbey. Another Prime Minister whose
tomb is in the south transept, is Lord Melbourne (died 1848), Queen
Victoria's tutor in statesmanship – 'as for the confidence of the
Crown', she wrote, 'God knows, no *Minister*, no *friend*, EVER possessed it so entirely as this truly excellent Lord Melbourne possesses
mine!' And there is a third, too, commemorated by a tablet – Lord
Palmerston, who died in 1865 and was buried in Westminster Abbey.
Both Melbourne and Palmerston, related by marriage, lived and died
at Brocket Hall in Lemsford.

The Brocket Chapel contains the tombs of earlier owners of the
Hall, chiefly the seventeenth-century Brockets and the eighteenth-
century Reades. Elsewhere in the church are buried John Barnet,
Lord High Treasurer, who died in 1373, and Cardinal Louis of
Luxembourg, who died in 1443. In a corner of the churchyard is a
picturesque half-timbered house, once the *Baker's Arms* inn.

This rapid tour has of necessity left a good many churches unde-
scribed; may I hope that my readers will fill the gaps for themselves?
Discovery is always more satisfying than direction. Where, for
instance, is the church in which German airmen of the First World

War are buried? Where is the church in whose tower is a stone to a young man hanged in 1758, who 'begged a grave in this church-yard'? Where is the church with a memorial to James Janeway, Puritan divine and author of a book for children that asks its young readers 'How know you but that you may be the next child to die'? Where is the church that houses the Adam and Eve tomb?

CHAPTER SEVEN

Some Inns

Time was before the coming of railways or, earlier, of adequately surfaced roads, when London lay at a day's journey from Hertfordshire, so that all travellers to Scotland or the North had to put up for a meal or two, more likely for a night's lodging, at one or other of the county's numerous inns. Though as far back as 1577 an Order in Council, recording 527 licensed premises in Hertfordshire, might say that 'as we find some of the keepers of those inns and alehouses of good wealth so do we find the greatest number of them very simple houses and the inhabitors of them very poor', only 20 years later Elizabeth I's Surveyor General, John Norden, declared that 'no Shire in England for the quality comes near it for thoroughfare places of competent receipt' and early in the next century John Taylor (whom I may be allowed to quote more fully than in my first chapter) was even more comprehensive – 'for good clean highways, conscionable short miles, meat, drink, lodgings for travellers, kind men, women fair and honest, and with everything that is necessary this county is plentifully stored withal'. Each of these estimates was, of course, correct – in 1577 there certainly were good, some already ancient, inns at St Albans, Ware, Royston, Berkhamsted and other highway towns, of which a couple of dozen survive (though rebuilt) today. There were middling inns on roads of lesser importance, whose numbers grew with the increasing ease and popularity of travel. But there were also – and at all periods – alehouses and beerhouses so small that they could be run by the wife while her husband earned his living elsewhere. Curiously enough, the advent of the motor-car has enormously enhanced the prestige of certain survivors of these last, converting them from insignificant cottages into popular resorts with cocktail bars, dining rooms, car parks and all the rest of the paraphernalia. I can think of one (not untypical of a good many more), almost the only house within a mile in any direction, which boasts a regular clientèle in both bar and dining room from a radius of 20 miles or more.

But travellers were not by any means the inn's only reason for existence. At one time Quarter Sessions were held in a Hertford inn, sectional meetings of Justices at inns in various parts of the county and Petty Sessions at the *White Hart*, Welwyn, for at least 50 years down to 1900. The earliest mention of the *George and Dragon* at Baldock records the holding of an Archdeacon's court there in 1591. Turnpike Trustees met at inns along the roads for which they were responsible; so too did lords of the manor presiding over their manorial courts; so too did coroners down to the Licensing Act of 1902, which forbade them to continue 'if other suitable premises have been provided' – 'the coroner', said Dickens, 'frequents more public houses than any man alive'. Occasionally – as at the *Royal Oak*, Hemel Hempstead – the inn was also for a period the local lock-up. All sorts of official village events, and quite as many unofficial jollifications, took place at the inn; the parish Vestry, having met in the church, as often as not adjourned to one or another of the locals; and in town and village alike a fair number ran benefit clubs that were the forerunners of today's great Friendly Societies.

Again, from the inauguration of a postal service in the sixteenth century inns might serve as centres for letter collection and distribution; they also sometimes housed the local Inland Revenue office or Excise office. They were the usual scene of political meetings and (even today sometimes) of auction sales – and at three Hertfordshire inns schools were held: the *Three Horseshoes*, Norton, Letchworth, from the 1840s to 1873, the *Bridgewater Arms*, Little Gaddesden, in the 1850s and the *Brocket Arms*, Ayot St Lawrence, a Sunday school from 1940 to 1958. The intimate connection from medieval times between inn and theatre has been too often described to need further comment; suffice it to say that inns at St Albans, Hitchin, Hertford, Ware and other places all had their assembly rooms in which touring companies performed during the eighteenth and nineteenth centuries, and that in a barn behind the *Wheatsheaf*, Watford, the young Henry Irving appeared in 1856 as a member of Holloway's Portable Theatre. Wilson Barratt was a later performer in the same barn – which, by the way, is no more. The quite modern *Hilltop* at Hatfield has a hall and stage and at one time ran regular Saturday night variety shows.

For all who are interested in social history, therefore, inn hunt-, ing can occupy many fruitful weekend outings – after all, Hertford-shire can boast a total of roughly 860 inns, big and small, whose licence is more than a century old. And here it will be well to make plain one vital fact – that the age of an inn (the age that I shall quote) is that not of its building (revealing though this may be) but of its licence. Today, the exigencies of a town-based, highly mobile and affluent society, plus the ham-handedness and in moments vul-garity of a good many brewers' architects, are too often transform-ing what used to be genuinely picturesque inns, evidences of their history thick upon them, into something that is, at best, neither flesh, fish, fowl nor good red herring. The point is that even in a 1970 monstrosity the visitor may, in fact, be on historic ground. It is practically never possible to determine the exact year in which an inn first opened its doors; well, so be it. That licensed premises have stood on the same site for a century, perhaps for many cen-turies, is surely enough.

The inn-hunter in Hertfordshire can, of course, set off from any point he chooses, sure of his reward. For myself, I begin at Welwyn and for two reasons – the immediate district contains interesting inns and, secondly, exploration based on the Great North Road can be made in three different directions.

Welwyn's oldest inn is the *Wellington* (before 1816 the *Swan*), kept in 1352 by John Strayler – it may also have been the inn men-tioned in the records of the manor of Welwyn Rectory in 1298, when a landlord unnamed was in trouble 'because his wife has sold common ale as a special brew.' At every brewing of ale, by the way, the landlord had to give the Rector (who was also lord of the manor) one gallon, one pottle and one quart of best ale, for which the Rector paid a ha'penny. In later centuries Pepys stayed there at least once – 'very bad accommodation at the *Swan*', he commented. Refaced in 1725, it was known both to David Garrick and almost

31 *New River monument, Chadwell Spring, Hertford*

32 *Milestone, 1732, at Bar*

33 *Iron bridge, Gadebridge Park, Hemel Hempstead*

certainly to Dr Johnson.

Not far away, the *Rose and Crown*, which changed hands in 1633, was Welwyn's first post office. At the further end of the village the *White Hart*, established about 1675 and enlarged about 1760, stole all the local coach trade and also sheltered for a night the body of Lord Byron on its way to burial in Nottinghamshire in 1824.

A couple of miles southward from Welwyn and slightly west of the road is Lemsford, with the curiously named *Long Arm and Short Arm*, rebuilt shortly before the Second World War – the name derives from the position of the house, on the site of a blacksmith's forge and cottage, at the junction of the pre-1833 line of the Great North Road and the short switch road then built to connect the village with the new.

One personal memory of the *Long Arm and Short Arm* deserves rescue from oblivion in these schedule-ridden days. In the 1930s London Transport ran a late-night bus, small and rather ramshackle, from St Albans to Codicote, which reached Lemsford almost exactly at closing time. Drawing up outside the inn, the driver never failed to disappear into the bar in search of his regular passengers, shepherding them to their seats on board with unfailing good humour. Whether the bus were late or not at its destination didn't in the least matter; the human warmth and benevolence of life had been preserved and everyone was happy. The bus no longer runs, alas; and even if it did, I fear that the driver would have his eye on the clock rather than on his passengers.

At Hatfield are two inns worth notice – the *Red Lion*, opened in 1794 and much enlarged in recent years, at one time having 120 acres of land attached to it; and the little *Eight Bells* at the bottom of Fore Street. In 1837 the fire at Hatfield House drew among the newspaper reporters who flocked to the scene the young Charles Dickens; and a year later, in *Oliver Twist*, he made Sykes, in flight after the murder of Nancy, reach Hatfield and take refuge in what, from Dickens' description, must have been the *Eight Bells*. A bit self-conscious of such adventitious notoriety, the house has, as a matter of fact, a perfectly good claim to attention in its own right, as a

relatively little altered early seventeenth-century, one-storey building with dormer windows in the roof.

Between Hatfield and Potters Bar, however, there is only a single
inn, and that a modern one. At Potters Bar itself the *White Horse*
and the *Lion* both belong to the eighteenth century. Just short of
the county boundary, the elegant *Duke of York* (modern excresc-
ences can be ignored) was built in 1811, possibly replacing a much
older inn, the *Angel*.

Returning to Welwyn and continuing north along the Great North
Road (now demoted to B 197), at Woolmer Green a turning eastwards leads to Datchworth. On Datchworth Green is the eighteenth-
century *Tilbury*, its name and licence transferred about 1838 from
the inn mentioned in the previous chapter, standing in a corner of
Datchworth churchyard and owned by the parish. Not far away, on
Bulls Green, the weatherboarded *Horns* (the weatherboarding covering a timber frame of probably the sixteenth century) was the scene
in the late December of 1782 of a night-long countryside rejoicing
in the death of a local footpad named Walter Clibborn, who had
just been shot a short mile away and whose body lay in a shed beside
the inn. At dawn it was buried by the roadside where he had died,
with a stake driven through it – a replacement of the stake is there
today.

The sequel, however, is not without significance. The farm
labourer, who admitted firing the fatal shot, was tried for murder
and acquitted; his master, who had ordered him to fire it, was
presented with a silver cup by the Lord Lieutenant. Safety on the
roads was evidently considered to be of greater importance than a
straining of justice.

On the southern outskirts of Stevenage is the *Roebuck*, now a
motel attached to an older, but heavily restored, half-timbered
house. There was certainly an inn here well before 1670; but it
chief interest lies in its fairly well-authenticated association with
Dick Turpin. The net closing round him, Turpin hid at the *Roebuck*
arranging to meet his wife secretly at a small Hertford alehouse
On arrival there, however, the first person he clapped eyes on was
a constable carrying his staff of office; whereupon, discretion exceed

ing hope of connubial felicity, he galloped off (but not on Black Bess) to Yorkshire, where he lived under his mother's name of Palmer and was hanged in 1739.

In Stevenage itself the partially rebuilt *White Lion* receives its earliest mention in 1659, when the landlord, William Welch, was stated to be seven years in arrear with his rent. In Napoleonic days prisoners of war on their way to the great internment camp at Norman Cross in Huntingdonshire regularly slept under guard in its barns and outhouses. In Stevenage too the *Red Lion* is of much the same date at the *White* ditto, though much nearer its original state; and in the New Town the *Twin Foxes* commemorates in its sign two local poachers, identical twins named Albert Ebenezer and Ebenezer Albert Fox (sons of a local preacher) who assuredly foxed the magistrates with their alibis for many years and died round about the 1920s.

And so, through Graveley, to Baldock, a town for centuries devoted to malting and brewing. Here the *George and Dragon*, considerably rebuilt but still with some fragments of older work, received George Fox, founder of the Quakers, in 1665, watching him pacify and, as he tells us, reconcile two customers fighting on the premises; ever afterwards the *George* was a sure port of call for travelling Friends. In later centuries the wife of a footpad called Shock Oliver, hanged at Hertford in 1808, is said to have brought his body to the *George*, where she was a cook, hiding it until it could be taken on for burial elsewhere. At Baldock too the *Rose and Crown*, *Chequers*, *Cock* and *White Lion* all go back to the seventeenth century; and the *White Horse* stands on the site of what was for long Baldock's leading inn of the same sign, much frequented before its closure in 1864 by followers of the Puckeridge Hunt, among them the *Punch* artist, John Leech, who demanded a horse 'on which you can carry an umbrella in a hailstorm'.

From Baldock it will be convenient to visit Ashwell, both for the attraction of the village and for the interest of its inns. The sixteenth-century *Rose and Crown* was probably an inn long before its earliest mention as such in 1746. In the 1790s it was owned by a Baldock brewer named James Ind; his brother, Edmund, moved from

Baldock to Romford, Essex, where in the course of time he took as partners W. O. E. and G. Coope. At the *Three Tuns* a branch of Barclay's Bank still opens on one afternoon a week; and the little *Engine,* tucked away in a back street, was formerly the *Engine and Drum,* the drum being a regional name for a threshing machine. In the 1850s the landlord used to operate one by means of a 5 HP engine.

Now, returning a second time to Welwyn, consider the road to Hitchin. At Codicote the *George and Dragon* is, so far as I have discovered, Hertfordshire's oldest licence. Here in 1279 – virtually 700 years ago – Laurence the Taverner ruled over a house unnamed in any extant document but by 1481 called the *Greyhound.* What kind of house it may have been one can only guess, although, conspicuously situated alongside the medieval market place, it may well have been imposing for its time. Nor is it known when the sign changed to the *George and Dragon* – perhaps at the rebuilding soon after 1550. Here in 1745 recruits from a great part of Hertfordshire mustered to defend the county against the threat of the Young Pretender.

The next inn is not met until St Ippollitts, a mile south of Hitchin. Close to the hilltop church there is the *Olive Branch,* a picturesque timbered house with massive brick chimney, said to date from the sixteenth century but an inn from only about 1850. On second thoughts, however, I now realise that I was hasty in pressing on to the *Olive Branch;* at Little Armshoe the roadside *Royal Oak* is shown on a map of 1766, though the house appears to be older; and just before reaching St Ippollitts a gaunt late Victorian erection bearing the sign of the *Greyhound* has, in fact, been licensed premises for two centuries.

As the focal point of north Hertfordshire Hitchin has always and inevitably been well furnished with inns, a fair number of which have mercifully survived ruthless changes in the town of recent years. Pride of places goes to the *Cock* (which once gave its name to High Street), probably medieval in origin, rebuilt in the sixteenth century but almost completely modernised since and at one time much larger than it is today. About the *Red Hart,* without doubt one

of Hertfordshire's most picturesque inns, nothing appears to be trace-
able since its building four centuries ago. Of the same period too is
the *Sun*; but that has accumulated memories galore.

There it was that the town bull and boar were housed – and at
one time the fire engine; that Parliamentary troops were quartered
in the Civil War; that all official gatherings – Archdeacons' courts,
manorial courts, petty sessional courts, Vestry meetings, Turnpike
Trust meetings – were held, and later the meetings of the Hitchin
Friendly Institution; that the Hitchin Volunteers had their headquarters during the Napoleonic wars. In its eighteenth-century
assembly rooms the Hertfordshire-born Georgian star, Harriett
Mellon, made her theatrical début with a touring company in the
opening years of last century; she became in turn wife of the
fabulously rich banker, Thomas Coutts, and Duchess of St Albans.
In its yard was once a chalybeate spring frequented by seekers after
health. And somewhere about its exterior walling is a brick on which
three highwaymen scratched the date, 1772, when they held up the
landlord and all his guests.

Only two other Hitchin inns must detain us. The *Cooper's Arms*
at the top of Tilehouse Street is a fifteenth-century house, possibly
at one time the meeting place of the tilers' or brickmakers' Guild.
It was certainly owned in 1750 by the Hitchin brewer, William
Lucas, but there is no clear indication of a licence until a century
later.

The second is outside the town, on the road to Little Wymondley.
It is the *New Found Out*, partly seventeenth-century in its building
and at one time the Hitchin pest house for small-pox sufferers but,
so far as can be determined, first licensed little more than a century
ago. There was once a *New Found Out* at Ashwell – what does the
sign mean? I have never met a satisfactory explanation.

So far the inns briefly mentioned are to be found in the middle of
Hertfordshire; inns on highways east and west of them call for no
less attention, beginning with those along A 11 on the county boundary with Essex.

A 11 enters Hertfordshire at Sawbridgeworth, where the *Hand
and Crown*, the *Old Bell*, the *White Lion* and (despite its name) the

George IV all date from the early eighteenth century, with the *King's Head*, formerly the King of Prussia and before that the *Crown*, a couple of decades later. So too does the *Greyhound* at Spellbrook, half way to Bishop's Stortford, in its early days having a blacksmith's shop attached and a turnpike gate opposite.

In all market and thoroughfare towns of any continuing vigour the survival of inns is a chancy business, especially in these planning days. Bishop's Stortford is no exception. Yet there are still enough ancient licences to justify a visit, even without the long-vanished *Reindeer*, in Pepys' time a notorious brothel ('and all the good fellow of the county come hither'), or the recently closed *Grapes*, whose ex-licensee was hanged in 1903 for the murder of three wives. The *George*, for instance, reprieved in 1965 from a threat of demolition, is an amalgam of the seventeenth, eighteenth and nineteenth centuries; yet as far back as 1417 it was owned by Nicholas Coleman, who was succeeding Thomas Petworth, while its day-to-day management remained in the Hawkins family from then until about 1700. Charles I dined here in 1629 and again in the following year; and in the 1820s (when it was also the Excise office) Henry Gilbey, father of the Walter Gilbey who founded the well-known distilling firm, drove a daily coach from the *George* to London and back. The *Star*, the *Black Lion* and the often photographed *Boar's Head* were all at work by the middle of the seventeenth century; in the suburb of Hockerill the *Cock* saw the funeral of its landlord, Thomas Browne, in 1648, while Richard Thompson set up a post office at the *Coach and Horses* in 1771.

The great Roman road to York, later called Ermine Street and now A 1010 and A 10, has carried at some time or other pretty well every famous character in history. Yet famous or not, they needed refreshment and lodging. A good many of its roadside inns (some of the most interesting too) have been closed in recent years; but enough remain to satisfy the most exigent inn hunter.

On the county boundary at Waltham Cross, the *Falcon* was the *Roebuck* in 1617, changing its sign not long after – in the 1860s and 1870s it was the *Great Eastern Hotel*. Only a small house in its early days, it developed the popular post chaise business during the eighteenth century and throve on it – a James Pollard print of 1832 shows it with a pillared Georgian gateway and pedimented door alongside, a house of six bays and in parts of three storeys built round a courtyard, some new, some plainly old. Spanning the road was a gallows sign, similar to the one still outside the recently closed *Four Swans*, a house of even earlier origin.

Among Cheshunt's older inns are the *Haunch of Venison* (the *Vine and Castle* in 1669), the *Ship* (1734), the *Woolpack* (1756) and the *Old English Gentleman*, probably named after its owner, George English, in 1785. At the *George* an early landlord is said to have been the Stevenage-born James Whitney, afterwards an enterprising highwaymen hanged at Smithfield in 1694. The *Roman Urn*, opened about 1800, has an urn, reputed to be Roman, incorporated in its front wall. Somewhat away from the main road, the *White Horse* at Flamstead End was the *White Horse* in 1589, in 1662 'formerly an inn called Copt Hall afterwards the *Crown* and lately the *White Horse*'; in 1701 the *Ship*; and the *White Horse* again half a century later. At Turnford the *Old Bull's Head* may be the inn kept in 1603 by Robert Trimmer, whose 'wife is a notorious slut, his daughter a common naughty-pack'.

A little higher up the road, the *Bull* at Broxbourne was owned by the Convent St Mary, Bishopsgate, London, in 1521; the *White Bear* (mentioned in 1643) had a remarkable line of female licensees, all of the same family, from 1761 to about 1956. Between Broxborne and Hoddesdon is the *Golden Lion*, probably the *White Hind* in 1590; but at Hoddesdon itself the finest inns, the *Bull* and the medieval *Maidenhead*, were demolished in the early 1960s. All the same, the *Salisbury Arms* and the *Swan*, nearly side by side, were receiving guests in mid-sixteenth century; in the nineteenth both had gallows signs. The *Salisbury Arms* (formerly the *Black Lion*) was in its day the post office and the Excise office; and in 1807 its housekeeper, a Mrs Hummerstone, was murdered by the rejected suitor of a maid-servant. Elsewhere in Hoddesdon the *Bell* was a going concern in 1684; but the *Thatched House*, to which Izaak Walton 'was wont to repair for my morning cup of ale' and which stood rather nearer the road junction, vanished about a century ago.

And so, past the *Duke William of Cumberland* (in 1570 the *Cock*, kept by Alice Godeskirk or Cokkey) and Great Amwell, to Ware, like so many other towns the graveyard of notable inns. But still surviving are the *Star*, mentioned in 1512 and the *Old Bull's Head*, from which 'Robert, a servant, a stranger' was buried in 1572. The *Angel* appeared for sale in 1631 and the *Bell* dates from the same period. The *Wine Lodge* was the *Vine* in 1659 and the *Waggon and Horses* the *Coach and Horses* in 1664 – three years later than the earliest mention of the *Spread Eagle* at Amwell End. And finally, of course, the little *Bell and Sun* – the *Hatblock* in 1669 (its owner was a hatter) and in succession the *Maidenhead*, the *Charing Cross* (named after its then owner), the *Angel*, the *Vine* and in mid-eighteenth century the *Sun and Bell*.

But the most interesting inn of the town is the *French Horn*, a house (behind its Victorian frontage) dating from about 1630 with a fine staircase and dog gate. As an inn, however, it cannot be traced before 1738, when it was described as no longer a dwelling house. An enlargement made in about 1770 included an assembly room in which, among other touring players, Ellen Tree, afterwards wife of Charles Kean, and Edward Stirling played.

Adjoining Ware on the west is Hertford, as county town a natural focus of inns, though having now lost many of its best. But not all – the *Blackbirds* was the *Pye* in 1607 and the *Magpye* later in the century, when Thomas Ashfield was ordered to be whipped 'from the Blue Coat School to the *Magpye* Inn'. The *White Hart* and the *Ram* are both listed in a survey of the town made in 1621, while the *Old Ship* claims to date from 1643 and the modern *Woolpack* was in fact the *Half Moon* soon after 1700. In 1785 the *Three Tuns* in St Andrews Street was established in what had previously been a parish workhouse; but the attractive mid-eighteenth-century *Blue Boy* close to the Bluecoat school is not mentioned as an inn until 1809, though it may well have been one earlier. Of rather more recent date (and even then rebuilt about 1966) the *Duncombe Arms* celebrates Thomas Slingsby Duncombe, the only Radical ever to represent Hertford in Parliament – from 1826 to 1832.

One inn, however, is of special interest. The *Salisbury Arms* (before 1820 the *Bell*) accepted a Hatfield man as lodger for life in 1431 – its cellar still shows medieval masonry, though the rest of the house, round a now built-over courtyard, is of the seventeenth century, with a good Jacobean staircase. In 1642, at the outbreak of the Civil War, it was the scene of an attempt to raise men for the King in a town that had just imprisoned its Royalist mayor; a few years later Cromwell is said to have lodged in it. County Justices in Quarter Session met there for a short period, as did many other official bodies more regularly, and it was the inevitable meeting place of townsfolk on all great occasions. A busy coaching inn, it was from the *Bell* in 1814 that £5,000 in notes and securities, duly locked and sealed in a box, set out for London, only to arrive empty but with seal intact and lock untampered with. The ingenious thief, a man named William Cooke, received the astonishingly light sentence of seven years' transportation.

And now back to A 10. North of Ware, the *Sow and Pigs* at the entrance to Wadesmill may have earned its name from an eighteenth-century card game said to have been popular with farmers, My Sow's Pigg'd; formerly it had been the *Five Horseshoes* and the *Fox*. In Wadesmill itself the large *Feathers* was 'newly called the *Prince's Arms*' in 1615; at one time it had a gallows sign and stabling for 100 horses, and the village fair used to be held in the meadow behind the house.

Reluctantly passing several small inns on the way, our attention is next called to the *Crown and Falcon* at Puckeridge, an interesting building dating basically from about 1530; the inn is an amalgamation of the *Falcon*, on the present site, with the former *Crown* higher up the village. It was at the *Falcon* that Pepys stayed in 1662 'much cramped by my new hard boots' but buying a pair of shoes from the landlord – 'and so rid in shoes to Cambridge'. Also in Puckeridge the early sixteenth-century *White Hart* had a landlord in 1728, a former Excise man named Bradley, who was imprisoned for counterfeiting coins. A short mile eastwards the broad street of Standon contains the *Old Bell* (the *Wellhouse* in 1646) and the *Star* of half a century later.

Some miles to the north the *Old Black Bull*, probably functioning in 1673, and the *White Hart*, mentioned in 1600, are Buntingford's oldest inns since the closure of the very ancient *George and Dragon*, where Pepys' wife was once taken violently ill through drinking cold beer on a hot day. But the curious will risk a short trip to Hare Street, near Great Hormead, to spare a glance at a bleak red-brick Victorian house bearing the sign of the *Jolly Butchers*. Here stood the *Dog's Head in the Pot* in 1594 – there was also a *Dog's Head in the Pot*, or *Dog and Pot*, in Bishop's Stortford down to the 1890s and a map of 1611 calls Hare Street Dogshead. Under that strange sign the inn continued until 1760, when it was owned and kept by Jeremiah Smith, a butcher; it was his daughter Abigail who renamed it the *Three Jolly Butchers*. Who the other two may have been is anybody's guess.

On the county boundary Royston (where Ermine Street enters Cambridgeshire and becomes A 14) can boast of its *Bull*, an owner which died in 1520; the present drab brick frontage gives no clue to the older portions in rear. In its comfortable dining room (and with the bar not far off) Petty Sessions were held in the early nineteenth century – and continued to be held, in spite of increasingly peremptory orders from the powers that be, down to 1883, when they were transferred to the newly built police station. Royston has lost several of its most handsome inns; but there remains the *Chequers*, fairly tactfully restored, to which Leonard Huett was licensed in 1618. In the late eighteenth and early nineteenth centuries the *Green Man* housed the, for that time, extremely liberal-minded Royston Dissenting Book Club, one member of which was Henry Crabbe Robinson. And at the *Coach and Horses* the landlord of the 1840s once allowed a well-known local Chartist to hold forth on his premises; he was threatened by the magistrates with loss of his licence if it happened a second time.

From London to Chester in Roman days ran Watling Street; no doubt it was lined by Roman inns and it would be pleasant to be able to prove that at least one or two existing licenced premises in its Hertfordshire stretch were in fact of Roman origin. But as well might one cry for the moon, even though the precise dates of their first opening remain unknown. Ancient many of them are, more ancient possibly than one suspects; let it rest at that, with no encouragement to fantasy.

At Watling Street's southern entrance to the county, Elstree, the *Old Holly Bush*, an inn by 1786, appears to be a fifteenth-century house, though much altered; it may quite likely have been the late medieval church house, where both ecclesiastical and lay functions were held. At the *Artichoke* (kept in 1750 by Philip Coghill) the inquest was opened in 1823 on the body of William Weare, a notorious gambler and bad hat, murdered at Gill Hill (nowadays a most respectable neighbourhood) by John Thurtell, son of the Lord Mayor of Norwich, Joseph Hunt and William Probert.

The murder itself was merely sordid and brutal; what makes it worth recalling is the blood-lust that convulsed the whole country when the crime became known and the three men were arrested. Newspapers – not excluding *The Times* – devoted daily columns to assuming their guilt even before trial. Tens of thousands of crude broadsheets inflamed minds unreached by the scarcely restrained Press. At least two London theatres staged melodramas the sole attraction of which lay in the employment as stage properties of some of the accessories used in the commission of the crime. The cottage at Gill Hill rented by Probert was thronged by sightseers (the landlord making a pretty penny out of them), who in a short time had stripped every tree of its last leaf as souvenirs. Little wonder that, after a trial at Hertford lasting two days, Mr Justice Parke broke off his summing up to denounce 'the prejudice which has been raised against both the prisoners through the Press, of which they have both complained and which nobody can gainsay': both prisoners, not three, because Probert had turned King's evidence and been discharged. Hunt was sentenced to a long term of transportation and Thurtell was hanged at Hertford (by an executioner who was drunk) before a crowd estimated at 15,000 people.

Through Radlett and Colney Street (the *George and Dragon* and the *Red Cow* both in existence in the mid-eighteenth century) we come to Park Street, with the *Falcon*, licenced in 1618, whose landlord in 1775 made over all his goods to a local pawnbroker, together with a letter: 'Be so good as to acquaint my wife that I am safe in London.' In Park Street too is the *White Horse*, established a few years before 1689.

And then St Albans. A book, not a few paragraphs, would have to be devoted to St Albans inns past and present if their stories were to be fully told. Many, prosperous in their day, have vanished. Of the survivors some, though old in licence, tantalisingly conceal much of their histories. Others are relatively modern, though still with points of interest. A fair number have been converted to different uses. From the Middle Ages, when St Albans was a place of national pilgrimage situated on a great national highway, it has been thronged with inns; only a dozen out of three times that number in the City today can be given more than a bare mention here.

It will be well, even if ungracious, in the first instance to dispel a persistently fostered St Albans legend – that the much photographed *Fighting Cocks* down by the river is one of England's oldest inns. Sweet are the uses of advertisement; the sad truth is that, originally a corner turret or rear gateway in the wall that surrounded the conventual buildings of the medieval Abbey (which of course accounts for its shape) it became an inn only in 1600, when it appears to have been known as the Round House. At what date a cockpit was installed is uncertain; additions were made to it from time to time, some of which were later demolished. In the course of a poaching case in 1855 it was referred to as the *Fisherman* beerhouse.

A number of old or oldish inns, about which there is little to say but which merit notice all the same, are the *Bell*, mentioned as long ago as 1452, the *Old King's Arms*, 1633, the *Rose and Crown* at St Michaels, 1635, the *Hare and Hounds* in Sopwell Lane, 1672, the *Boot*, 1719 though the building is older, the *King's Head*, 1745, the *Peacock*, in Hatfield Road, 1756, and the *Duke of Marlborough* shortly before 1800.

Stories of others, however, can be told if only in outline. The *Fleur de Lys*, for instance, was built, probably as an Abbey guest house, round about 1430 on the site of a house traditionally said to have been occupied for a time by King John of France after his capture at Poitiers in 1356 and on his way from Hertford to Berkhamsted Castle. During the sixteenth and seventeenth centuries it was virtually rebuilt round a courtyard – and again in the eighteenth, its granaries, haylofts, coach-houses, stabling and grounds (including a bowling green) stretching over what is now Verulam Road. Its prominence in the town might no doubt have been greater had not the *Red Lion* sprung up to blanket it off from the busy highway of Watling Street, which then ran up Holywell Hill, along the present High Street and down George Street.

The *Red Lion* may have been a fairly new house in 1556; it was owned and run for a century and a half by a leading St Albans family, the Selioks, who provided several Mayors and more 'principal burgesses' – that is, Aldermen. In 1613 Anthony Seliok was fined for using 'disdainful and opprobrious words' against a prominent townsman; and at an election in 1685, Colonel Sir Winston Churchill being one of the candidates, another Seliok was alleged to have 'threatened the innkeepers and alehouse keepers that if they did not give their voices for Lord Churchill their licences should be taken away from them'. In the yard of the *Red Lion* early in 1643 Cromwell arrested the High Sheriff of Hertfordshire, Sir Thomas Conyngsby, who was attempting to rally the town to Charles. The earliest lodge of Freemasons met there in 1739. In the late eighteenth century and for most of the nineteenth the inn had an underground stable for ten or a dozen horses; but it vanished together with the rest of the old premises on a rebuilding in 1896.

Two existing inns have associations with the two battles of St Albans during the Wars of the Roses, in 1455 and 1461. The first is the *Queen's Hotel*. It stands on the site of the very ancient *Chequers* (which still gives its name to the street); it was 'between the *Key* [the *Cross Keys*, now demolished] and the *Chequer*' that the Yorkist forces broke into the town in 1455. In 1828 the *Chequers* was done away with by a new and sporting licensee, Thomas Coleman, who built on the site the *Turf Hotel*, with hot baths, a news room and billiard room, all extremely up-to-date amenities at that period, as well as elaborate outbuildings in which theatrical touring companies regularly performed. He also instituted the St Albans Steeplechases, which continued for nine years and are commemorated in a James Pollard print showing the exterior of the *Turf* and a noble collection of horseflesh. Coleman's fortune, however, appears to have changed; he is next heard of as running a small Tap in rear of the *Turf*, which had itself become in part a straw-hat factory, in part the *Queen's Hotel*. It was at the *Queen's* that Dickens stayed for a time when he was writing *Bleak House*.

The second inn is the rather unobtrusive *Cock*, an earlier building on the site of which is said to have been a dressing station at the second battle of St Albans in 1461 – Hatfield Road was for centuries called Cock Lane. The present building, apparently seventeenth century in date, used to have a floor of human bones, a fragment of which is still preserved. But at what period it became an inn is conjectural – I have found no completely reliable reference to it as such until 1756. A century ago a guest in the house was 'General' Tom Thumb, an American named Charles Sherwood Stratton, born in 1838 and dying in 1883; he was 31 inches high and married a girl of 32 inches.

The diversion of Watling Street – that is, the southern entrance to the town – from St Stephens to Sopwell Lane and the later diversion from Sopwell Lane to the London Road, both of which I described in my third chapter, affected two old inns in particular. The *King Harry*, opposite St Stephen's, was a going concern in 1505 when it was bequeathed by the owner to his son and was 'named and bearing the figure of King Henry', – that is, of Henry VII. How long it had already been in existence there is no means of telling – its advantageous site might suggest a very early date. Had the road switch to Sopwell Lane deprived it of much of its old custom, so that it must henceforth rely on the far less busy Hatfield–Reading road (turnpiked in the eighteenth century) between St Albans and Watford? Nowadays it has a pleasant Georgian frontage concealing a much older rear portion.

It was, on the contrary, the building of the present London Road in 1794 that made the fortunes of the *Peahen*. Mentioned in 1480, this was the traditional scene (unsupported by the smallest evidence) of a secret marriage between Henry VIII and Anne Boleyn – then and for centuries later a small timber-framed house overshadowed by the much larger *Woolpack* next door. But when it came to occupy a conspicuous corner site its owners and landlords, the Marks family, were able in time to seize their opportunity; by 1852 the *Woolpack* had been absorbed and in 1897 new premises took the place of the old, incorporating, however, ceiling beams and other medieval fragments. It was at the old *Peahen* that the inquest was held in 1819 on the victim of a race through Redbourn between the Holyhead and Chester coaches, in which the Holyhead coach was overturned. The two drivers (said to have been kept in irons for six months before their trial) were each sentenced to a year's imprisonment.

Other early inns that must, alas, be hurriedly passed over are the *Goat* in Sopwell Lane, already in licence in 1598 and with a common lodging house attached to it in the nineteenth and early twentieth centuries; the little *White Lion*, bequeathed by its owner, Thomas Browne, in 1594; and the picturesque *Six Bells* at St Michael's, 'le Bell' in 1596 and probably changing its sign when the neighbouring church increased its peal about 1739. A Directory of 1826 calls it the *Ringers* – bell-ringing is thirsty work. But more demands to be said about the *White Hart* on Holywell Hill.

Holywell Hill was formerly pretty well lined with inns, the *White Hart* being the sole survivor. First built as a guesthouse of the Abbey, it is said to have had a chapel for the saying of Low Mass, though a lease of 1535 (the last granted by the Abbot) makes no mention of it. Twenty years later the house was described as 'formerly the *Hartshorn*'. Owned and sometimes run by a succession of Mayors and 'principal burgesses', it shared with the *Red Lion* the beneficent and profitable smile of the Corporation as a meeting place for junkettings and official occasions – such as that in 1761 : 'By cash expenses at the *White Hart* on meeting of the Aldermen and Officers to proceed to declare war upon Spain 7s 6d.' The war was, of course, the Seven Years' War, which had in fact broken out six years earlier – the year in which, incidentally, the *White Hart* was recorded as having stabling for 50 horses. A drawing of 40 years later shows it with a plastered Georgian frontage extending up the hill beyond the present archway; but after a fire in 1803 this frontage was piece by piece removed at various times, the last vestiges disappearing shortly before the Second World War, when the whole house underwent a good deal of restoration. There is still, however, some original panelling, a handsome staircase and a mural decoration not in its old position.

Here it was that the persistent troublemaker, Lord Lovat, was lodged after capture in 1745 on his way to London and execution and was painted by Hogarth. Engravings of the portrait sold like hot cakes; the portrait itself, said to have been found 80 years later 'in the house of a poor person in the neighbourhood of St Albans', is now in the National Portrait Gallery. But in 1770 the inn found itself, so to speak, headlined in news of a very different sort, when the *Gentleman's Magazine* reported at some length the divorce proceedings of Lord Grosvenor against his piquantly pretty wife (painted by Lawrence) who, it was shown, had been guilty of 'criminal conversation' at the *White Hart* with the Duke of Cumberland, brother of George III. At this distance of time the evidence is faintly amusing. The 'mistress of the White Hart', Mary Langford, declared that the bed in Lady Grosvenor's room looked as though it had been sat on but not lain on; another witness, however, commented on the rumpled state of the bed and disorder in the rest of the room. Lord Grosvenor's butler, Matthew Stevens, admitted that he had bored two holes in the door – 'to listen through' – later breaking into the room (when the Duke fled, leaving Lady Grosvenor to face the music) and clearly seeing the impression of heads on the pillows. The Duke's 'porter' admitted that his master was for the occasion, dressed plain like a country farmer'. The Duke had to pay £10,000 for his pleasures.

So long has been spent – I hope profitably – at St Albans that little time is left for inns beyond it. Passing the rebuilt *Punch Bowl* (the *Bole* in 1639), the narrow street of Redbourn contains three inns – the *George*, the *Red Lion* and the *Saracen's Head* – all dating in their licence from the sixteenth century, as well as the *Holly Bush* at Church End. But older than any is the *Bull* behind its very commonplace frontage; in 1595, when William Finch took possession, it was stated to have been previously owned by his father and

34 *Aldbury*

35 *Codicote, the George and Dragon*

'before that by Finches from ancient times'. In the coaching era it was a stage for all vehicles from London to the North-west; and two of its early nineteenth-century licensees, Henry and then his widow Catherine, were parents of Dr Henry Stephens (born 1796), close friend of John Keats (who stayed here in 1818) and inventor, for purely personal use, of Stephens' blue-black ink. Later he was persuaded to give up his medical career to exploit this invention commercially.

One more inn and one only – the *Sun* at Markyate Street – must be allowed to detain us. The present *Sun* is an amalgamation of two inns, the *Sun* and the *Cross Keys*; it was at the *Sun* in 1605 that the servant of Ambrose Rookwood, one of the conspirators, was arrested after placing horses ready to relay news of the success of Gunpowder Plot. Two centuries later Thomas Pickford, member of the pioneer road haulier family, presided over the St Albans Turnpike Trust at the *Sun* and the *Bull* in Redbourn alternately.

From St Albans, by the way, a short round trip may be made to Harpenden, Wheathampstead and Sandridge.

At Harpenden the *George* was mentioned in a will of 1509. The *Old Cock* has had an intriguing variety of signs – the *Cock* in 1637, the *Bell* in 1676, the *Cock* again in 1728, the *Sun* soon after, once more the *Cock* in 1799 and the *Old Cock* since 1906. An advertisement in 1914 says 'Beanfeasts catered for' – it would scarcely, I fancy, apply today. The *Old Bell* and the *Marquis of Granby* were both in existence in mid-eighteenth century.

Interesting in its associations is the *Cross Keys* (the *White Hart* in 1731), the licensee of which in the 1830s, an ex-huntsman named Henry Oldaker, was concerned with his brother, Robert, in establishing horse races on Harpenden Common that continued down to 1914, the condemnation of which by Cussans I quoted in a previous chapter. It is only fair to add, however, that in later years their reputation improved greatly.

One of the most photographed of all Hertfordshire inns is the *Bull* at Wheathampstead, the greater part of its building dating from the seventeenth century – recent modernisation has not made the problem of dating easier. Tradition declares that it was a fishing

resort of the Abbots of St Albans; but since the medieval manor
of Wheathampstead was held by Westminster Abbey, with whom St
Albans carried on bitter strife for several centuries, tradition may
very well be doubted. In 1617 there were 119 acres of land attached
to the *Bull*; it was the post office in the eighteenth century and a
favourite refuge for Lord Northcliffe and the actor, Sir Henry Beerbohm Tree, in the early twentieth.

A mile north of Wheathampstead, at Gustard Wood, the *Cross
Keys* stood in 1613 and the curiously named *Tin Pot* received a
certain Nicholas Brooks, who had been refused by the *Bull*, in 1655.
On the home run, between Wheathampstead and St Albans, at
Sandridge, the *Green Man*, the *Queen* and the *Red Lion* all date from
the early eighteenth century, though the house in which the *Queen*
is situated is pretty certainly older.

In the west of Hertfordshire A 4141 and (after Hunton Bridge)
A 41 are basically Roman roads from London to the North-west; in
1762 they were turnpiked, but what is known of the inns along
their route shows that they were recognised as a highway a long
time before that. In recent years, however, local development has
combined with brewery mergers to close and often demolish a
considerable number of the most interesting of those inns and it is
relatively few of the remainder to which attention need be drawn.

Bushey, for instance, not long ago closed its oldest inn, leaving
only a very small handful of fairly recent establishments. Notice,
however, the *Horse and Chains* – more properly the *Horse in
Chains*; from it horses used to pull wagons up the steep hill
opposite, the last horse entering into well-earned retirement as late
as the 1920s.

Much the same process of closure has been at work in Watford;
there was a time when its narrow winding High Street contained a
dozen or more inns, big and small. The principal one, the *Essex
Arms*, was demolished in 1928; in 1966 the dignified Georgian building of the *Rose and Crown*, at the corner of Market Place and
Market Street, was demolished and the inn transferred to new and
smaller premises, with no dignity at all, a little distance away.
Nevertheless its licence has been continuous since before 1557, when

t was owned by Merton College, Oxford. One of its licensees, by
he way, John Rogers, who died in 1829, was said to 'outrival in
ize and weight the famous Daniel Lambert'; it was during his
enure that a parcel handed to him for delivery in London, was
ound to contain the dismembered body of a young girl. It was
ent as directed; but the recipient was afterwards given a long term
or body-snatching, the actual snatcher remaining undiscovered.

Several other Watford inns of some age appear, as these lines
ire being written, under sentence of closure and are therefore,
hough reluctantly, omitted. Some miles northwards, King's Lang-
ey is justly proud of the *Saracen's Head*, a going concern in 1613
ut suggestively situated alongside what 20 or more years earlier was
:nown as Drunkard's Lane – moreover, one of its ceilings still has
Tudor badges in plasterwork. The *Rose and Crown* and the *Red Lion*
vere both wine taverns in 1633.

A little further on, Boxmoor, with several inns, must, alas, be
ieglected in favour of Hemel Hempstead, where the *Rose and
Crown* was occupied by Richard Patwyn in 1523. A century later
he *White Hart* was next door to the vicarage and the *Bell* was also
unctioning – in mid-seventeenth century it was owned and
occupied by a surgeon, who carried on his practice from it and stored
iis drugs in the beer cellar. The *King's Arms*, an amalgamation of
wo former inns, though much restored, is a seventeenth-century
iouse, its yard being occupied a century ago by the local straw-
plait market. The *Royal Oak* (as was said earlier in this chapter)
vas once the local lock-up; both the *Fishery Inn* and the remote
Three Horseshoes* at Winkwell drew much of their trade from the
Grand Union Canal (opened in 1800) at a time when barges were
iorse-drawn.

Like most highway towns, Berkhamsted was always well pro-
rided with inns old and new. The oldest still surviving is the *Bull*,
old to a certain John Woodhouse in 1535; the *Swan* and the *Queen's
Arms* are mentioned in 1607. But the most storied inn, as well as
he largest, is the *King's Arms*, probably established, however, under
Queen Anne and for some centuries the centre of Berkhamsted
ictivities – Vestry meetings, Turnpike Trust meetings, Petty Ses-

sions, local society meetings, balls and social gatherings of all sorts
not forgetting a vociferous meeting in 1833 to protest against th
coming of the railway. In the nineteenth century it was the Inlan
Revenue and the Excise office and in the eighteenth the post office
ruled over for 40-odd years before his death in 1840 by John Page
then by his widow Mary. In the early years of the century it wa
haunted by the exiled Louis XVIII of France, in residence nea
Aylesbury, who developed a close friendship with Page's daughter
Polly; on his restoration to the throne in 1814 she paid a deliriou
visit (platonic) as his guest at Versailles. In 1841, when Quee
Victoria and the Prince Consort changed horses at the inn, John'
daughter, Sarah, was so overcome by the occasion that she died o
a heart attack just as a loyal address was being presented.

A little beyond Berkhamsted, the *Crooked Billet* at Northchurch
though recently rebuilt, dates from before 1753 and the *George an
Dragon* from 40 years later. At Wigginton the *Cow Roast* was for
merly the *Cow Rest*, having large cattle pens in which drover
from the Midlands rested their beasts on the way to London markets

At the entrance to Tring the picturesque *Robin Hood* is a dis
appointment, in that, though the building is plainly seventeent
century or even earlier, next to nothing of its history as an inn ca
be traced. In the town itself the *Bell* had a licensee, Henry Gery
in 1611, of whom it was officially said that 'he hath been drun
since Christmas'. But it is the *Rose and Crown* that claims most o
our attention.

In the hands of Thomas Robinson in 1620, it was even then
prosperous house. Later it prospered further as a coach stage. Fo
many years it was the Excise office and in 1852 the booking office o
the London and North Western Railway, though the station is
full mile off. Bought in 1872 by Lionel Nathan de Rothschild o
Tring Park, it was rebuilt by his son, the first Baron Rothschild, ir
1906, partly to house the overflow of guests, hunting and otherwise
in the big house, and its visitors book contains many famous names
But it was the older *Rose and Crown* that will be recalled by ad
mirers of William Cobbett as the scene of a great dinner to him ir
1828, at which, in spite of a cold which nearly robbed him o

speech, he made a trenchant attack on the Government. 'As I declared in parting, for many, many years I had not spent a happier day.'

But what of the scores – nay, several hundreds – of inns away from great thoroughfares, in villages and along country lanes? Some are surprisingly large for their rural situations and handsome in their various styles – to pick at random (in addition to many of those described earlier in this chapter), the half-timbered *Old George* at Ickleford, the *Bull* at Whitwell, the *Bull* at London Colney, the *Red Lion* at Stanstead Abbots, the *George and Dragon* at Watton, the *Buck's Head* at Little Wymondley; of later periods the *Baker Arms* at Bayford, the *Greyhound* at Aldbury, the *Red Lion* at Water End, Great Gaddesden, the *White Horse* at Hertingfordbury. Others are small, sometimes thatched, sometimes weatherboarded cottages – the *Catherine Wheel* at Albury, the *Cock* at Stocking Pelham, the *Three Tuns* at Great Hormead, the *Bell* at Cottered, the *Three Horseshoes* at Hinxworth, the *Plough* at Sleapshyde, near St Albans. It will no doubt be noticed that the majority of them lie in the eastern half of the county; inns in the western half are on the whole less attractive in aspect though not in history.

So many others have points of interest that, once again, only a random sample can be made. The *Bell* at Benington, for instance, displays an early eighteenth-century wall painting in its bar. At Ridge the *Waggon and Horses*, formerly lying in wooded country well away from the highway (which was re-sited in 1826) was a fairly well-authenticated resort of highwaymen. The *Land of Liberty* at Rickmansworth commemorates the cooperative settlement established there in 1846 by the Chartist M.P., Fergus O'Connor, but declared illegal and sold nine years later. The *Old Red Lion* at Much Hadham (the *Angel* in 1577) contains a cupboard behind the fireplace, with shelves stepped back to fit the flue, in which the body of a girl was once found, no doubt the victim of some forgotten village crime. A deed of 1757 concerning the *Three Horseshoes* at Garston, near Watford, now at a busy road junction, speaks of an orchard of 76 trees immediately surrounding it. The sign of the *Mop and Brooms* at Shenley recalls a traditional battle between locals and gypsies in which these weapons were used. In the *Bell* at Widford, Charles Lamb sat when he revisited Blakesware, demolished in 1822. And at the *Fox and Hounds* at Barley (until a few years ago the *Waggon and Horses*) the gallows sign was taken from an ancient thatched inn of the same name, also in Barley, burnt down in 1950.

For about 60 years from 1490 the Stanley family, Earls of Derby, owned a manor at Whitwell. Their crest was, and is, an eagle carrying a child – and at Whitwell there is still an *Eagle and Child*. The earliest mention of it does not occur until rather more than a century after their departure, when it bore the same name as today. But the house itself, or part of it, certainly dates from Stanley times; it was enlarged in 1747. Was it first opened as an inn by a Stanley retainer or a villager anxious to acknowledge his landlord? There was once, by the way, an *Eagle and Child* at Ware – again on Stanley land – but it has long since disappeared.

The chances by which early mentions of an inn are obtained are intriguingly illustrated at Watton, where the first mention of the *Bull* is found in the parish register of baptisms for 26 February 1608: 'Edward Penefather, son of Ralph and Marion, was baptised, of Aston, but was delivered at the *Bull* in Watton as she passed by from market.'

CHAPTER EIGHT

Hertfordshire at Work

It is no doubt a truism that the basis of life is work: without work there is no survival. A chapter may therefore be fittingly devoted to noting some relics of Hertfordshire at work in past centuries – apart, that is, from its whole landscape, that vast palimpsest of the skill, tenacity, adaptability and devotion of generation after generation of men. An England that has become largely a land of town-dwellers, or of country dwellers with a townsman's mentality, seeing in the countryside little more than a playground for their pleasures, needs constant reminder that it is as vital, and as intricate, an industrial concern as the factories.

Through that countryside run the roads that I described briefly in my first chapter, carrying its finished products to their various markets, bringing back the finished products of the towns to its workers, a link without which no industry could continue – even primitive man had his trackways from settlement to settlement. There are, of course, other links as well, one of the most obvious of which to road-users are the railways – or what is left of them.

As I said, again in my first chapter, Hertfordshire's earliest railway was the London and Birmingham line through Watford, Berkhamsted and Tring, opened in 1838. Next, between 1840 and 1842, came a line through Broxbourne, Sawbridgeworth and Bishop's Stortford to Cambridge – originally, by the way, intended to run to York. Thirdly came the Great Northern in 1850, through Hatfield and Hitchin to Doncaster, with a branch from Hitchin by Royston to Cambridge in the following year; and lastly, in 1868, the Midland through Elstree, St Albans and Harpenden. In the extreme south-west of the county the Metropolitan Railway reached Rickmansworth in 1887 and Chorleywood a couple of years later. Meanwhile a network of small cross-country lines, all promoted by private companies before being taken over by one or other of the principal ones, ran hither and thither in no very organised fashion. Nearly all have been closed in recent years; but their relics – rusting rails, cuttings and embankments, picturesque red-brick bridges often allowing scant headroom, wooden or brick-built little stations now, alas, derelict – are thick on the ground. There are, however, more substantial railway monuments – if that is the word – which no motorist can miss seeing. Take, for instance, the county's several viaducts.

Much the best is at Welwyn, designed by Lewis Cubitt and built by Thomas Brassey between 1848 and 1850 – it is occasionally included among the notable viaducts of the country. Some 1,560 feet in length, it has 40 arches, the highest of which is 100 feet above the Mimram valley; and even today it carries only its original two tracks. The impossibility of increasing the number, both on the viaduct itself and through the tunnels immediately north of it, led later to the construction of the loop line from Stevenage through Hertford to Wood Green, on the northern outskirts of London, which itself has two good seven-arch viaducts, at Hertford and Cuffley respectively.

How the Welwyn viaduct came to be built is an interesting story. An early plan of the railway promoters took the line from approximately the site of the present Welwyn Garden City along the Mimram valley to Welwyn and thence, through the country around Kimpton, into the middle of Hitchin. I have heard the feasibility of this plan doubted by railway experts and in how much detail it was considered by its promoters I do not know; titled local landowners raised such an outcry at the proposed desecration of their estates (nobody troubled to inquire what the villagers of Welwyn thought of it) that it was abandoned forthwith and the present route by Knebworth and Stevenage, which involved a costly spanning of the Mimram, substituted. A brickworks was opened in the hillside adjoining the valley and cantonments for the navvies were built; but two winters of persistent frost hampered the work and it was not until early in August 1850 that the first train, filled with Directors and their friends, crossed it. A curious footnote to this is provided by the 1851 Census, wherein the return for Welwyn shows 16 British subjects, all the wives or children of railway workers of one kind or another, who were born in France; and I have heard elderly Welwyn folk tell how their grandparents remembered any number of 'foreigners' in the district. It is, of course, well known that many of the French railways were built by British labour.

Near Watford, and carrying the main line from Euston to Manchester and Glasgow, is a good five-arch brick viaduct over the Colne, the middle arch with a span of 40 feet and a height of about 35 feet. Originally (that is, in 1838) it carried two tracks but was widened in 1859 and again in 1875 and now carries four. Judging by the number of early prints, it was much thought of in its early days; I have one in which it dominates a verdant landscape threaded by a silver river, not as it is today, over a tatty valley rimmed by factories. In this respect it is less happily situated than the well-known Bushey arches, a mile nearer London and spanning the road complex between Bushey and Watford, which dominated a built-up area (not vastly changed from then to now) from the first. Bushey arches are again five in number, with rusticated stone facings. When in 1859 a third track was added to the original two it was laid on a separate steel structure leaving a gap of seven feet between it and the old; this gap was filled by the fourth line in 1875. The whole viaduct underwent modernisation in the early 1960s.

These viaducts apart, there are, of course, smaller railway bridges in Hertfordshire which, interesting though they are, cannot conveniently be seen from a car. But others can and should be. I choose six somewhat at random.

Just south of Berkhamsted station a small road leading past the castle to Potten End goes under a bridge, narrow in its west approach, of which the southern abutment makes an almost right-angle turn half way through the bridge's width, thus giving a far wider eastern approach; this is due, as with the Watford viaduct, to later increases in the number of tracks. Not far away, at Hemel

Hempstead, a brick bridge with a single 25-foot-high arch carries over Queensway the now closed line from Boxmoor to Harpenden. Above the arch is an earthen embankment; what is peculiar is that outside the wing walls, and apparently quite separate from the bridge itself, are narrow tunnels through the embankment for pedestrians. And at Harpenden, in the district known as Bowling Alley, is a fine single-arch skew bridge carrying the old Midland main line, of which the arch is ribbed and the abutments echeloned to take the skew.

St Albans can show what I personally regard as the most gracefully designed railway bridge in the county. It can be seen from London Road at the south end of the town and carries the Midland main line over a cutting of the closed branch from St Albans to Hatfield. Its single semi-circular brick arch rises to a height of 50 feet or more and is flanked by massive buttresses that do but emphasise the lightness of its spring – a most satisfying sight. Not, however, that it is the largest single-arch bridge that Hertfordshire can boast of – a road bridge near Knebworth golf course over the main line out of King's Cross has a span of 96 feet and a height of 48 feet.

On the east side of the county are two worth a passing attention. Along A 10, roughly halfway between Puckeridge and Buntingford, an iron girder bridge over the closed St Margarets–Buntingford branch has superimposed on it a skew bridge carrying the road. And at Slip End, to the south of Ashwell, is a curious three-arch brick bridge on the Hitchin–Cambridge branch, in which the middle one of the three segmented arches has been reinforced by a semicircular arch built inside it.

Finally, in our very haphazard dealings with railways, the changed sites of three important stations may be noted. The first Hertford East station, built in 1843, stood at the bottom of Railway Street; the new one, with its heavy brick and stone portico (and incidentally a couple of most attractive fluted iron columns holding buffer lights from the old), took its place in 1888, the last remnants of the old disappearing about 1964. At Watford in 1858 the present Junction station replaced an original one just north of the bridge carry-

ng the St Albans road; and at Berkhamsted the 1838 station at the
end of Castle Street – a sham-Elizabethan erection – gave way to the
present more austerely designed building in 1875.

For a thousand years before railways, however, another link
between country and town had been the utilisation of waterways.
Hertfordshire is without a river of any size and the Lea alone could
be so used, though only at some hazard; not until London had developed into an almost insatiable market were steps taken to enable
both it and the Stort to contribute substantially to the county's
prosperity. And then, at the turn of the eighteenth century, came
the Grand Junction Canal (now Grand Union Canal) intertwining
with the Colne, Gade and Bulbourne, concerning itself less with
Hertfordshire than with long-distance traffic but not without assistance to such towns as Hemel Hempstead and Berkhamsted. Watford,
from which it was separated by the mansion and park of the Earl
of Essex, benefited least of all.

Now at this point – and with a lack of logic worthy of a better
cause – I propose to deal shortly with a waterway designed and
constructed for a very different purpose.

Towards the end of the sixteenth century Hugh Myddelton (afterwards knighted), Alderman of London, M.P. for Denbigh and a rich
mineowner, undertook at his own expense to provide an additional
water supply for London, the City Corporation, although well aware
of the urgency, refusing to tackle the job themselves. Myddelton
tapped a rich spring at Chadwell, between Hertford and Ware (it
can be seen in the valley below the Hertford–Ware road, A 119),
and another just below Great Amwell church. From them, and
following the contours, he dug a channel some 40 miles long (since
a good deal shortened) to Clerkenwell, whence the water was con-
veyed, at first in wooden pipes, to adjoining parishes; nowadays it
debouches into large reservoirs at Manor House, near Finsbury
Park. But less than half way through the work Myddelton's money
ran out; the Corporation still refused to advance a penny and the
whole enterprise might have collapsed had not James I lent what
was necessary on the security of half the eventual profits. In 1613
the New River, as it was called, was formally opened; six years later

the New River Company was formed. But not until five years afte
Myddelton's death in 1631 was it able to show a small profit – by
which time Charles I, tired of waiting, had exchanged the Roya
Moiety, the name borne by his father's loan, for a fee-farm rent
The money so released was divided as King's Shares among the 3(
existing 'Adventurer' shareholders; whereupon profits increased and
share prices began to rise, then to soar, then to rocket – an investor'
dream of paradise – maintaining fantastic values over two full cen
turies. Single shares changed hands at various times for 5,000
guineas and £8,000 – and money had a vastly higher value in those
days – and Cussans reported that 'at a sale held in May 1873 fou
sixteenths of a King's share were sold by the trustees of the late
William Astill Esq. at an average price of £3,060 each. During the
previous year each sixteenth was entitled to a dividend o
£112: 3: 2d.' When in 1904 the New River Company as a wate
undertaking was absorbed by the newly formed Metropolitan Water
Board it was still left with immensely valuable land and building
along the full length of the River; these it still, for the most part
holds, paying in 1969 a dividend of 13½ per cent or 2s. 8.4d. pe
share.

By the early eighteenth century, when London expansion de
manded more and more water, Chadwell spring showed signs o
drying up; whereupon the Company obtained powers to let ir
water from the Lea, building a gauge to measure the amount – i
can still be seen like a white sarcophagus over the cut made from
Lea to New River. In 1856, however, it was supplanted by a new
gauge on the Lea bank (the towpath between Hertford and Ware
passes it) – essentially, a sluice controlled by a gate connected to
two iron boats which rise and fall with the river; it is said to be
the only one of its kind in the world. The average daily inflow from
the Lea is 22½ million gallons.

Along the Hertfordshire stretch of the waterway are six yellow
brick pumping stations, all now electrically operated (though one
preserves an early-nineteenth-century Boulton and Watt engine)
the oldest, on Amwell Hill, dating from 1847. It is crossed at various
points by 19 road bridges and a number of footbridges; ten of the

road bridges have been rebuilt in recent years but the remainder, all iron-girdered, date for the most part from the first half of the nineteenth century, the earliest, carrying a side road from A 10 on the outskirts of Ware to Great Amwell, bearing the date 1824.

Waterways are obviously better seen from the deck of a cruiser than from a car; but the motorist can still catch many glimpses of them – of the Grand Union Canal along A 412 around Rickmansworth and A 41 north of Watford; of the Lea Navigation along A 119, A 10 and A 1010; of the Stort Navigation along A 414 and A 11. Probably the most rewarding in its variety is the Grand Union Canal, threading its way through a tangle of lakes south of Rickmansworth, playing leapfrog with the Gade and the Bulbourne north of Watford, fed by four very large reservoirs (wonderful wild-life sancturies) near Tring, crossed by 44 road and five railway bridges and with a total of 38 locks. When it enters the county at Rickmansworth it is 127 feet above sea level; at Tring, beyond which it enters Buckinghamshire, it is 382 feet – a rise of 255 feet in 20-odd miles and the highest point along its roughly 200-mile route. Though its best-known beauty spots are elsewhere, it passes in Hertfordshire through scenery for the most part charmingly rural, in moments verging on the squalid, but never featureless; and near Tring it crosses the crest of the Chilterns in a picturesquely tree'd cutting $1\frac{1}{2}$ miles long and between 20 feet and 25 feet deep. Its numerous bridges vary in interest from the brick-built and steeply-humped one adjoining Stockers Lock near Rickmansworth, which plainly dates from the Canal's first opening, to the concrete construction alongside the *Fishery* Inn, Hemel Hempstead – not, of course forgetting the little timber-decked swing bridge at Winkwell, not far from the last named, only ten feet wide and prohibited to loads over two tons. In a good many, evidence of early building, in brick abutments and wing walls, remains in spite of later iron-girdered decks replacing the original brick arches. The masonry of all the locks dates from the Canal's opening, though always pretty heavily patched; but lock gates have to be renewed about every 40 years. Nowadays canal users operate the locks themselves; but lock-keepers' cottages, occupied by maintenance staff or let to private persons, are fairly common. In recent years, however, the gaudily decorated narrowboats that used to enliven the scene with so much fascinating colour have virtually disappeared, replaced by trim white-painted cruising craft occasionally (but only occasionally) manned by crews nearly as gaudy in their holiday apparel as the old narrowboats.

A word on the Canal's history. Begun in 1793, it was opened as far as Braunston, Northamptonshire, in 1800. The first threat to its soon established success came with the London and Birmingham Railway in 1838, which crossed and recrossed it for many miles north of Watford; but for nearly half a century the Canal Company refused to acknowledge defeat. This it further staved off by successive amalgamations with similar Companies in the Midlands, finally, in 1929, securing unified control from the Thames to the Trent and changing the name of the entire waterway from the Grand Junction to the Grand Union Canal. Then in 1948 it, like all others in the country, was taken over by the British Transport Commission and in 1963 by the British Waterways Board, with a regional office in Watford.

The British Waterways Board also controls the Lea and Stort Navigations. The first Navigation in 1739 cleared the Lea of its shoals, flashes and other obstructions but did little else; in 1765 John Smeaton made a series of new cuts, created a continuous towpath and increased the number of locks. So the Navigation continued until 1868, when it was taken over by the Lea Conservancy Board, which made over the years further improvements to meet the demands of heavy traffic, the last being the enlargement of the channel during the First World War to take ships of 100 tons as far as Hertford. Then, in Hertfordshire at any rate, traffic dwindled catastrophically and has now ceased, except for pleasure craft. A trip down the Lea from Hertford to its junction with the Thames at Blackwall is a thrilling experience, embracing all types of scenery from the placidly rural to the gigantically industrial, with small areas of desolation in between. The middle reaches are unlikely to be greatly changed in the coming years by the creation of the Lea Valley Regional Park.

One bridge in its Hertfordshire stretch is of curious construction. It joins Broxbourne to the Essex village of Nazeing. From the Nazeing end the road rises on a long ramp of brick arches, to be joined at the top of the rise by two side-roads, also ramped, one from Broxbourne Mill on the south, the other from open land on the north. Thence it crosses the Lea; then, after a dog-leg turn, a piece of waste ground; then, after another dog-leg, first, the railway from Liverpool Street through Bishop's Stortford to Cambridge, and, second, the New River; and finally emerges on to high ground beyond Broxbourne station. Narrow throughout, it is made more difficult to negotiate by high parapets and, however curious in itself, should be approached only with circumspection.

'Placidly rural', the phrase I used to describe the upper reaches of the Lea, applies to the whole length of the Stort Navigation, established in 1766 to encourage Bishop's Stortford's malting trade but, in the event, going off at half-cock because of its failure to tap the rich barley country beyond. Whether for this reason or from persistently incompetent management, it appears never to have been commercially successful, passing from Navigation Company to private owner and back to a new Navigation Company – until finally, in 1911, the existing Company sold the entire undertaking to the Lea Conservancy Board for five shillings. To cruise through its long pounds in lush green meadows right down to its junction with the Lea near Hoddesdon is indeed to let a fretful world pass out of memory, the New Town at Harlow, just over the Essex border, being sufficiently far off to be more or less ignored.

Several times in this book the importance of malting in Hertfordshire's past economy has been stressed; nowhere is it more manifest than in the Lea and Stort valleys, where Hertford, Bishop's Stortford and, above all, Ware once led all England in that subtle industrial craft. But malting was by no means confined to the Lea valley; malthouses – practically none now used as such – are to be found all over the county, apart from the extreme south, in towns, villages and even isolated farms. They may be found nowadays serving as factories and workshops, as showrooms and stores, as offices, as village and church halls, as the headquarters of local organisations, as private houses; one is part of a laundry and another some years ago was a boarding home for cats. But at Ware, the heart of the industry, whose skyline once revealed literally several score, practically all have been demolished, Ware's present output being secured by two enormous ones built in 1905 (and much enlarged since then) and 1967 respectively. At Stanstead Abbots one nineteenth-century malthouse is still working, at Bishop's Stortford one, at Baldock four; but the most spectacular malting site is at Sawbridgeworth, where nine large malthouses, all owned by the same firm, stand end to end over a distance of some 350 yards, with three or four more immediately in rear. Yet even some of these are now used as garages and workshops.

Recognition of malthouses, whether still in use or not, can be a pleasant – as well as, in Hertfordshire, a significant – game, once the player knows enough of their purpose and structure to distinguish them. Malting is the process of converting barley into malt for the brewing of ale; the addition of hops in the brewing converts ale into beer; heavily kilned malt is the basis of stout. But before kilning the malt must be allowed to germinate, its starchy ingredients being prepared to be turned into sugar by fermentation. It is control of that germination that constitutes the whole art of the maltster.

Though for the most part picturesque buildings – quite as picturesque as, but far less popularly acclaimed than, the oasthouses of Kent – malthouses are severely functional in design. At one end is the barley store, where the grain is received from the farmer. Next, but invisible from the exterior of the building, comes the cistern in which, after screening to remove dirt and so on, it is steeped. After steeping it lies for some time in what is called the couch, where the first onset of germination is accompanied by a slight rise in temperature and the emission of carbonic acid gas. Then – and this provides the malthouses with much of their characteristic shape – it is spread over the malting floors (one, two or three above each other, each seldom more than six feet high), where germination continues for between one and two weeks in a temperature controlled by trimming the rows of louvred windows on both sides

37 *River Lea at Ware, old malting in background*

of the floor; these rows of windows, often small, in the long, sleek section of the building are the first feature to look for. But a word of caution: in malthouses adapted to other uses the low floors have sometimes been reduced in number or ripped out altogether to give greater headroom and the fenestration correspondingly changed.

The second, and quite as unmistakable, characteristic is the dome of the kiln and its surmounting cowl, usually in these days a flat iron plate called a mushroom. Generally speaking the dome itself resembles a truncated sugar-loaf; but a more modern type, sometimes combining the vents of two adjacent kilns, is no more than an ordinary tiled or slated roof at right angles to the malting floors, its cowling consisting of two or three rows of louvred metalwork. It is in the kiln that, when germination has proceeded to the desired point (a matter of highly skilled judgment), the grain is slowly heated, formerly by a fire of hornbeam faggots (commonly found in Hertfordshire), more recently by anthracite and sometimes by electricity, until malt of the desired quality is obtained. The floor on which the roasting grain rests is usually of porous tiles, though it used at one time to be made of woven iron wire. Lastly, the malt is allowed gradually to cool before being transferred to bins in the malt store beyond the kiln while awaiting delivery to the brewer.

Players of this game will, I think, find most malthouses pretty well intact even if somewhat disguised. But I have seen malting floors without their kiln and kilns without their malting floors; and at Braughing all that remains of a former malthouse is a single wall separating the road from a private garden. Its row of windows, though now bricked-in, gives away its original purpose completely.

It was Ware Urban District Council that some years ago demolished Hertfordshire's most intriguing malting site, the main building dating back to the early seventeenth century, though nothing definite is known of its use as a malting until many years later. And it was the Baldock Urban District Council that demolished in 1968 and 1969 Hertfordshire's finest brewery, a handsome early nineteenth-century yellow-brick structure, crowned by a clock turret, that lorded it over the wide High Street of that pleasant little town. Its loss left of county interest only the eighteenth-century

58   *On the Grand Union Canal near Boxmoor*

mansion of Benskin's Brewery, Watford, once the home of a forme
brewer, now the Company's offices. A delightfully rural little
brewery at Furneux Pelham, typical of a score of others that were
operating a century ago, has recently become a bottling store. A
handsome yellow brick one at Ashwell, dating from the 1830s
stands empty at the moment of writing.

Time was, and not so long since, when Hertfordshire could claim
a dozen or more windmills; several have since either fallen
down or been blown down. Its only post mill, quite likely two
centuries old and working until 1930, has been recently restored
sails, gear and all, though only as a landmark – it stands on high
ground at Cromer, near Ardeley, with a wide and undulating land
scape before it. Little Hadham's smock mill, built in 1770 and work
ing until 1929 is, however richly deserving restoration, unlikely, i
seems, to enjoy it. Brick built tower mills – all, I think, nineteenth
century in their building – are at Colney Heath, Croxley Green (con
verted into a house), between Reed and Royston, at Tring and near
Weston. A tower mill at Breachwood Green, King's Walden, is on
the point of collapse.

It goes without saying that flour-milling was for centuries an
essential industry in every county. But in the second half of the
nineteenth gigantic imports of grain from Canada and the United
States gave millers already established in the port towns the per
manent advantage over their county brethren of being able to silo
complete cargoes without the cost of inland transport by rail o
wagon. In addition, so far as Hertfordshire was concerned, a fall
in the water table was first noticed, which soon began to leave water
wheels with insufficient head to operate – some of them are now
high and dry. And even where they continued to turn, of course
the problem of transport remained – over and above which, few
millers had sufficient capital to install steam power. A directory of a
century ago lists 94 millers in the county, some working more than
one mill; today, only about 14 mills are still at work (some inter
mittently) on one kind of milling or another, including animal
foodstuffs and soya products; others are now engineering works o
warehouses, private houses or blocks of flats. The majority are brick

built and handsome at that; but a few are of the East Anglian type, weatherboarded on a brick base, with tiled or slated roof and the miller's house attached. Outstanding examples of this type are Picotts End Mill, Hemel Hempstead, where the house is dated 1783, and Moor Hill at Frogmore, south of St Albans, with a mid-eighteenth-century house. Kingsbury Mill, St Michael's, St Albans, possibly in its early days East Anglian in character, also has an eighteenth-century house. At the disused Noke Mill, Great Gaddesden, though the mill itself has been rebuilt, the detached miller's house, now in wretched condition, may possibly belong to the seventeenth century.

Nineteenth-century steam-powered mills (sometimes converted from water-power) include the very attractive Horns Mill and Sele Mill at Hertford, New Mills at Tring (with many twentieth-century additions), a large mill at Royston, another large mill at Ickleford and the rather handsome one at Standon (1900). But mill buildings, like malthouses, have always been expendable and some good examples of all types have been demolished in the last half-century. At Broxbourne a different fate overtook the mill in about 1950; it was burnt down when in use as an engineering works. What, however, was happily saved included a wall of sixteenth-century brick, with a little stone-cased window, and what almost certainly was a late seventeenth- or early eighteenth-century miller's house having a window of Regency Gothic design.

Little more than a dozen water wheels survive in the county, very few still in action and none of notable size – at Ashwell and at Charlton, near Hitchin, the wheel is pretty well all that remains of the mill. All except one are of iron but so heavily encrusted with chalk that their maker's name is untracable. One of the best – an outside wheel – is in the garden of a private house, formerly Sopwell Mill, St Albans; it has a diameter of 13 feet and a width of 6 feet 6 inches. Also in a private garden at Abbot's Langley are two wheels of a former mill, both between 12 feet and 14 feet in diameter and 14 feet wide. At Tonwell, north of Ware, the old millhouse, now a private residence and used as the Judge's lodging during Hertford Assizes, has fragments of a wooden wheel of, so it seems to me, unexpectedly light construction. Another wooden wheel, also incomplete, may be found on an island in the Gade near Hunton Bridge; probably of eighteenth-century date, it was later part of a pumping apparatus used to supply water to the mansion of Langleybury on the adjacent hilltop. Whether it ever belonged to a mill is a moot point.

Water power served also another early Hertfordshire industry, in these days chiefly exemplified by the giant works of John Dickinson and Co. Ltd, at Apsley Mill, Hemel Hempstead, Nash Mill and Home Park Mill in King's Langley and Croxley Mill at Rickmansworth, the first three alongside the Gade, the last by the Colne. Away back in 1495 John Tate was making paper beside the Lea at Hertford; but his enterprise does not seem to have survived his death and no more is heard of papermaking in Hertfordshire for a century and a half. Then, around 1650, it was made for a short period at Sopwell Mill, St Albans; by 1672 the Earl of Salisbury had established a paper mill at Hatfield which continued until 1838; and from 1713 to 1855 there was a paper mill at Standon, some of which still exists It was, however, chiefly in the west of the county that the industry expanded; during the eighteenth century five mills were established in the Rickmansworth area, five in the Hemel Hempstead area, one at Watford and one at Bushey, as well as shorter-lived ones at Sarratt, Redbourn and Wheathampstead. All these were water-powered. Most of them survived into the nineteenth century, Hamper Mill, Watford (now largely rebuilt as a private house), until 1908; but it was two in the Gade valley that made Hertfordshire famous in the industry.

Until the end of the eighteenth century paper was made in single sheets from rags shredded, pulped, firmly compressed and hung out to dry. Then two brothers, Henry and Sealy Fourdrinier, acquired a French invention for making paper much more quickly in an endless roll, calling in the engineer, Bryan Donkin, and a little later a Watford foundry worker, George Tidcombe, to devise, design and build the necessary equipment. Though the brothers went bankrupt, their work initiated all modern papermaking techniques and Fourdrinier machines, improved, of course, but basically unchanged, are universal.

All the early experiments of the Fourdriniers were carried out in two mills at Frogmore, a little south of Hemel Hempstead (not the Frogmore near St Albans) which they acquired in about 1803. One of these mills blew up some years ago when it was being used for a very different purpose; Frogmore Mill, now owned and operated by the British Paper Company Limited, was rebuilt in 1863. But for papermakers the site itself remains a hallowed one; and as though to keep alive the sacred flame the Company still employs at least one Fourdrinier machine made by George Tidcombe.

While the Fourdriniers were still at Frogmore there came to the nearby Apsley Mill, which had hitherto made paper by the old method, an enterprising young London stationer named John Dickinson. This he bought in 1809, immediately adopting the new invention – and improving it by inventions of his own. During the Napoleonic wars he was making a special paper for cartridges; as the years passed he was responsible for paper for early postage stamps and early envelopes, for the very special paper on which Government bonds were printed, and for many other lines of great importance and considerable profit, in addition, of course, to satisfying a constantly increasing demand for paper of all kinds brought about by the introduction of the penny post and repeal of the duty on newspapers.

Not content with that, he undertook much research into the chemistry of paper, introduced new basic ingredients and can rightly claim a pioneer's place in the development of the fine qualities of today. In 1811 he had also bought Nash Mill, where he lived for some years after his marriage; in 1826 he built Home Park Mill and in 1830 Croxley Mill. In addition he acquired three small already operating mills near Rickmansworth and kept them busy, too, though when the firm became a Limited Company in 1886 the last three were sold in order to concentrate production in the previous much rebuilt and greatly enlarged four.

Apsley Mill, alongside A 41, now covers more than 30 acres and, according to present plans, is due for a considerable remodelling of most of its nineteenth-century buildings; through the middle of the site but now conduited over, still runs the race that turned the old water wheel. Nash Mill and Home Park can also be seen from the road; Croxley, the second largest of the four, from A 412. Apart from the high standing of their products in modern British output they are significant as today's representatives of an industry that has existed in Hertfordshire for 500 years.

The last representative – not, technically speaking, in the direct line of descent – of another old Hertfordshire industry is the Kayser-Bondor Hosiery Mill at Baldock. A silk industry in the county is first heard of as already established at Watford in 1770. The earliest names associated with it are sturdily British; but it was soon taken over by a second-generation Huguenot, Pierre Paumier, who by the early 1790s was running three throwing and winding mills in the town; Rookery Mill alongside the Colne and two smaller ones, worked by horsepower, elsewhere. By 1807 he had been succeeded by his son-in-law, William Harty, on whose death in 1826 they were sold to at least two different owners. The smaller mills soon closed down but Rookery continued in production until 1881, when it was converted to other uses, only to be largely destroyed by fire in the 1950s and since partially rebuilt.

In 1806 Paumier or Harty, it is uncertain which, broke new ground by establishing a mill at Rickmansworth; it may be that the premises of a mineral water factory in High Street are part of it. How the Watford mills were manned I do not know; that at Rickmansworth employed at least a proportion of workhouse children. There was, however, nothing surprising in this; paupers of all ages and both sexes were expected in those days to earn what they could as an offset to the cost of their keep by the parish. The Rickmansworth mill, under a variety of managements, and still employing many children, but not latterly pauper children, closed down in 1889.

Two years before the Rickmansworth mill opened there came to Abbey Mill, St Albans, a John Woollam, who turned what had been a corn mill on the Ver into a silk mill, installing machinery that a contemporary writer described as 'constructed on a new and much improved principal'. At least two, possibly three, generations of Woollams worked there, adding large buildings to the original ones, changing from water-power to steam-power, and themselves living in the seventeenth-century millhouse just beyond the mill race. In 1906 Abbey Mill was sold to a London firm, who continued production until the outbreak of the Second World War and ownership until about 1955. The old mill has since been demolished, the newer buildings now housing several industrial concerns.

Imitating Harty at Rickmansworth, John Woollam soon opened a pauper-manned mill at Hatfield, which appears to have been still working in 1849 but must have closed very soon after; I have been unable to discover just where this mill was situated. To compensate for its loss a new steam-powered mill was built and opened at Redbourn; this, like Abbey Mill, was taken over by the London firm, continued until 1939 and is now incorporated in the large premises of a well-known tea and coffee importing company.

In Brook Street, Tring, the large mill now occupied by an engineering firm became a silk mill in 1824, finally closing in 1898; it had previously been a water-powered corn mill and still contains the county's largest wheel, 22 feet in diameter. The London silk firm of David Evans and Co., who operated it for the greater part of the century, almost completely rebuilt it in traditional mill fashion, though later work has somewhat modified the design; and in so doing they included a long single-storey building just inside the gates, now the engineering Company's offices, to lodge some of the 300-odd children they employed – who, believe it or not, were made to sing hymns while they worked and to sing more lustily than ever when visitors were shown round. One child working there in the 1830s was Gerald Massey, later known as the Chartist Poet, who is generally accepted as the model for George Eliot's *Felix Holt the Radical*. It may be added that Evans at some time or other occupied a second mill in Akeman Street, as well as operating with pauper labour a third at Aylesbury, Buckinghamshire.

A county directory of 1838 says that 'at St Albans, Watford, Rickmansworth and Tring about 1,200 persons of both sexes are employed in throwing and winding silk'. This does not take into account the brief experiment of John Ransom, a benevolent Quaker miller of Grove Mill, Hitchin. In 1826 he was described as silk throwster as well as miller; 13 years later as miller only. When the experiment failed, as it presumably did, he must have been thankful that he had not put all his eggs into one basket. He had rebuilt Grove Mill in about 1814; today it shows scant sign of either of its former uses.

Finally, a series of Victorian relics – if they can be called relics, since they are still in use – of both industrial and immense social significance may be briefly mentioned; the search for them can even, as I have suggested in other instances, be made into a kind of game. In 1853 the first pillar-boxes for letters were introduced into England after a short experiment in Jersey; design followed design as the years passed and some fascinating specimens of early ones are to be found in various parts of the country. The earliest in Hertfordshire, however, is outside the Town Hall at Hemel Hempstead; it belongs to a type made between 1879 and 1883 from which the royal cipher and the words 'Post Office' were carelessly omitted. An example of the succeeding type (with the same omissions), between 1883 and 1887, stands near the station at Harpenden. The only difference between them is that in the earlier type the postal aperture cuts the collar beneath the dome of the box, whereas in the later the collar remains unbroken. So far as I observed a year or two ago there are eight Victorian pillar-boxes still in service in the county, one or two in unlikely places – in the middle of an R.A.F. station at Bovingdon, for instance. There are also, by the way, four bearing the relatively rare cipher of Edward VIII.

Much commoner – about 80 in all – are wall-boxes, built into walls or brick pillars. The earliest in the county are two, installed only a few years after wall boxes had been introduced – one at Hexton, dating from 1860 and now in the wall of a post office rebuilt about 1913, the other at Great Gaddesden, placed there in 1861. There are four types of wall-box in all – or rather, to be accurate, three, with a 1960 modification of the third that may easily be mistaken for a different design. Between Codicote and Kimpton, by the way, is a wall-box inserted into the wall not of a post office but into what was once the lodge of the now demolished Kimpton Hoo. One of the principal aids in dating wall-boxes is that up to 1871 they were fitted with downshoot apertures often protected by a metal flap; after that date the aperture was an upshoot one, rendering protection from weather unnecessary and prying hands more difficult of insertion.

Lastly, what are known as lamp boxes – posting boxes strapped to lamp standards or wooden posts – were introduced in 1896; there are about eight left in the county, all in rural areas. Sorting out the different types of posting box and making a rough classification of their dates can be excellent fun.

Here I draw to a close. The plan I have followed – of my own devising, I confess – has forced me to omit aspects of the county, from schools to watercress growing, that I should have liked to discuss, as well as a host of personalities famous and infamous, grave and gay. I have tried to give, partially at any rate, my own birdseye view of what can be seen without difficulty in a small area of countryside that, because of the inescapable changes now, or soon to be, imposed upon it by outside circumstances, is urgently worth looking at. If I have encouraged readers to further exploration I shall be delighted; if I have persuaded them to the point of reading the more detailed studies of other writers (and there are plenty to be had, though being for the most part either available only in libraries or locally published, they are not easy to come by) I shall ask for nothing better. With that hope I conclude as the county's best-known local historian, the late Reginald Hine, used always to end his letters to fellow-workers, 'Yours in the love of Hertfordshire'.

39   *John Perient and his wife Joan (1415) at Digswell, from
a rubbing by R. J. Busby*

INDEX

The numerals in **bold** type refer to the page numbers of illustrations

A

Akeman Street, (A 4141, A 41) 23, 68, 72, 192
Albury, 195
Albyn, Robert, 159
Aldbury, 56, 77, 161, 195; **189**
Aldenham, 56, 156, 157
Almshoe, Little, 176
Amwell, Great, 150, 201
Andrews, Henry, 145
Anson, George, Lord, 122
Anstey, 20, 68, 93, 145
Ardeley, 58, 131, 146, 210
Argentein, John de, 93
Ashridge, 19, 107, 119-21; **18, 82**
Ashwell, 20, 21, 22, 44, 61, 72, 106, 130, 175, 200, 210, 211; **59**
Aston, Lord, 129
Atkins, Henry, 145
Auber, Harriett, 151
Aubrey, John, 125
Aylesbury (Bucks), 23, 215
Ayot, St Lawrence, 165, 169; St Peter, 34, 165

B

Bacon, Sir Francis, 116
Baker, Sir William, 127
Baldock, 16, 20, 21, 22, 24, 54, 56, 68, 70, 143, 169, 175, 206, 209, 214; **153**
Baldwin, Robert, 160
Barkway, 33, 145; **172**
Barley, 33, 145, 106
Barnet (Greater London), 23, 31, 80
Barnet, John, 166
Barratt, Wilson, 170
Bassyl, William, 108
Bayford, 127, 195
Beane river, 84
Becket, Sir Edmund, Lord Grimthorpe, 140-42

Becket, Thomas, Archbishop, 83
Beerbohm Tree, Sir Henry, 192
Beit, Sir Alfred, 128
Bell, Jane, 157
Benfield, Paul, 129
Bengeo, 151
Benington, 68, 92, 195
Benskin's Watford Brewery, 210
Berkhamsted, 20, 23, 27, 29, 38, 68, 80-4, 193, 197, 199, 201
Betjeman, Sir John, 156
Bishop's Stortford, 16, 20, 23, 29, 54, 68, 69, 80, 88, 148, 178, 197, 205, 206
Black Prince, 84
Blomfield, Sir Arthur, 148
Blount, Sir Henry Pope, 125
Bodley, G. F., 159
Bonner, Bishop, 89
Boreham Wood, 16
Boteler, Sir Francis, 108
Bodicca, Queen, 49
Bologne, Eustace de, 94
Bovington, 216
Bowcock, Richard, 164
Bowes-Lyon, Mary Eleanor, 132
Braughing, 22, 23, 34, 46, 52, 74, 146, 147
Brewing, industry, 209
Bridgewater, Duke of, 119, 127, 161
British Paper Co. Ltd., 213
Brook, Matthew, 160
Brookmans Park, 37, 122
Broughton, Urban, 120
Brownlow, Lord, 120
Broxbourne, 29, 69, 74, 151, 179, 197, 205, 211
Bruce, David, King of Scotland, 86
Bryant, John, 148
Buckland; **35**
Bulbourne, river, 43, 201
Buntingford, 23, 62, 69, 145, 182, 200
Burne Jones, Sir Edward, 146, 166
Burns, Major General Sir George, 114

Index

Bushey, 34, 56, 157, 192, 199, 212
Butler, Richard, 155
Butterfield, William, 159
Buxton, John, 102
Bygrave, 68
Byron, Lord, 173

Cromwell, Oliver, 87, 113, 181, 185
Croxley, Green, 34, 210
Cruden, Alexander, 150
Cumberland, Duke of, 188
Cussans, John Edwin, 74, 124, 150, 155, 156, 202

C

Caldecote, 61, 142
Calvert, Nicholson, 103
Capel, Sir Arthur, 130
'Carroll, Lewis', 111
Cary, Sir Henry, 103; Sir Robert, 103
Castle, Tom, 156
Cathcart, Lady, 128
Catherine, widow of Henry V, 86
Catuvellauni, 45
Charles I, 85, 102, 178
Charles II, 104, 126
Chaucer, Geoffrey, 84
Chauncy, Charles, 150; Sir Henry, 30, 131
Chesfield, 61
Cheshunt, 23, 29, 68, 102, 106, 107, 126, 152, 179
Chesshyre, Sir John, 92
Chipperfield, 124
Chorleywood, 32, 198
Christian, Edward, 151
Churchill, Lady Randolph, 126
Clarendon, Earl of, 125
Clibborn, Walter, 174
Clothall, 23
Clutterbuck, Robert, 157
Cobbett, William, 194
Cobbold, Lady Hermione, 116
Codicote, 29, 62, 72, 176; **189**
Coleman, Nicholas, 178; Thomas, 185
Colne, river, 72, 199, 201, 212, 214
Colney Heath, 210; Street, 183
Coningsby, Sir Ralph, 113; Sir Thomas, 113, 185; family, 115
Cooper, Sir Anthony Paston, 159
Cottered, 20, 61, 69, 131, 146
Cotton, Dr Nathaniel, 160
Coulton, G. G., 162
Cowper, Earls, 122, 128, 160; William, 160
Crawford, Mary Elizabeth, 158

D

Datchworth, 164, 174
Delmé-Radcliffe, 132, 163
Derby, Earls of, 196
Dickens, Charles, 115, 173
Dickinson, John, & Co. Ltd., 212, 213
Digswell, 21, 164; **218**
Dixon, Nicholas, 152
Drinking Fountains, 34
Duncombe, Thomas Slingsby, 180
Dunstable (Beds), 19, 22, 44

E

East India Company, 86, 129
Ebury, Lord, 122
Edgeworth, Maria, 128
Edmund, J. Langley, Prince, 98, 101, 158
Edward I, 105
Edward II, 97
Edward III, 88, 98
Edward VI, 87, 103
Elizabeth I, 85, 87, 103, 107, 109
Elizabeth, Queen, Queen Mother, 132
Elstree, 23, 183, 197
Ermine Street, (A 10, A 14) 23, 31, 43, 54, 68, 69
Essendon, 68
Essex, Earls of, 32, 122, 130, 157, 201
Evelyn, John, 109, 125

F

Fanshawe, Sir Richard, 150
Ferrers, Katherine, 124
Field, John, 147
Flamstead, 29, 123, 124
Flaunden, 158
Flaxman, John, 161
Fletcher, Rev. Richard, 148

Flint, Mary, 143
Forster, E. M., 15, 20
Fourdrinier, Henry and Sealy, 212
Fox, George, 175
Fox twins, 175
Frere, Prof. Sheppard, 50

G

Gaddesden, Great, 19, 161, 195, 211, 216; **17**; Little, 19, 121, 161, 169
Gade river, 43, 56, 201, 212
Gardiner, Edward, 131
Garrard, Apsley Cherry, 162
Garrick, David, 170
Garston, 195
Gaveston, Pier, 84, 97
Gee, Judith and Elizabeth, 156
Gibbons Grinling, 125, 161
Gilbert, Sir John, 133
Gilbey, Henry, 178
Gill, Eric, 147
Gilston, 127
Gimson, Ernest, 164
Glamis, Lady, 162
Godwin, William, 150
Goff, Richard, 147
Gore, Sir William, 123, 161; **99**
Grand Union Canal, 125, 201, 203; **208**
Graveley, 21, 61
Great North Road (A 1000, A 1, B 197), 23, 32, 43
Gregson, Bob, 124
Gresley, Sir Nigel, 126
Grimston, Sir Harbottle, 116
Grosvenor, Lady, 188
Gully, John, 124
Gwyn, Nell, 126

H

Hadham, Little, 130, 147, 210; Much, 20, 106, 129, 147, 195
Haileybury, 87
Hallard, Stephen, 164
Hallingbury, Little (Essex), 47
Halsey, Agatha, 161
Hare Street, 23
Harpenden, 29, 56, 74, 133, 191, 197, 200, 216

Hart-Dyke, Lady, 126
Hasty, William, 214
Hassall, Rev. Thomas, 151
Hatfield, 23, 27, 32, 34, 68, 107-13, 132, 165, 170, 173, 197, 212, 215; **41, 75, 76**
Hawkins, family, 178
Hawksmoor, Nicholas, 155
Hemel Hempstead, 16, 20, 23, 27, 29, 54, 72, 158, 169, 193, 199, 201, 203, 211, 212, 213, 216; **26, 136, 172**
Henry VIII, 86, 102, 107, 126, 186
Hertford, 27, 29, 64-8, 80, 84, 86, 122, 150, 180, 200, 211, 212; **66, 172**
Hertingfordbury, 61, 127, 195
Hexton, 22, 44, 216
Hinde, Robert, 163
Hine, Reginald, 217
Hinxworth, 130, 195
Hitchin, 20, 27, 56, 73, 132, 163, 176, 197, 198, 211, 216; **100**
Hoddesdon, 29, 32, 69, 151, 179
Hogarth, William, 188
Homestead Moats, 106
Hormead, Great, 182
Hoskins, Prof. W. G., 70
Howard, John, 85
Hunger, John, 86
Hunsdon, 102, 107
Hunt, Joseph, 183
Huntingdon, Countess of, 152
Hunton Bridge, 23, 125, 212

I

Ickleford, 22, 195
Icknield Way, (A 505), 22, 27, 45, 56, 68, 70, 96
Incent, Robert, 160
Ind, James, 175
Irving, Sir Henry, 169
Ivinghoe Beacon (Bucks), 19, 44

J

James I, 101, 107
John, King of France, 84, 86, 88, 184
Johnson, Dr Samuel, 157, 173
Jones, Inigo, 125
Jones, Rev. William, 152

K

Kayser Bondon Hosiery Mill, 214
Keats, John, 191
Kesteverne, William de, 155
Kimpton, 198, 216
Kit-Cat portraits, 127
Knollys, Elizabeth, 155

L

Lamb, Lady Caroline, 133
Lamb, Charles, 127, 133, 150, 196
Lambard, Simon, 148
Landscape, 15-20
Langley, Abbots, 56, 77, 211; Kings, 62, 96-101, 124, 158, 193, 212
Lawes, Sir John Bennett, 133
Lea, river and valley, 16, 27, 33, 43, 61, 69, 84, 127, 201, 202, 204, 212
Leech, John, 115, 175
Leeds, Duke of (Thomas Osborne), 114
Lemsford, 173; **190**
Letchworth, 16, 22, 44, 169
Leventhorpe, Joan, 149
Lilley, 22
London Coal Duty Boundary Markers, 37
London Colney, 34, 195
Louis XVIII of France, 194
Louis, Dauphin of France, 83, 86
Louis of Luxemburg, Cardinal, 166
Lovat, Lord, 188
Luton (Beds), 19
Lutyens, Sir Edwin, 114, 130, 144, 164
Lyde, Sir Limel, 165
Lyminge, Robert, 108
Lytton, Edward Bulwer, Lord, 114-6; Elizabeth Barbara Bulwer, 114, 164; Lady Emily, 114; Sir Robert, 114; Sir Rowland, 149

M

Macguire, Hugh, 128
Malting industry, 16, 32, 69, 205
Malthus, Rev. Robert, 88
Mandeville, Geoffrey de, 91
Marks family, 187
Markyate Street, 124, 191

Marlborough, Duchess of, 122, 133
Martin Brothers, 165
Massey, Gerald, 215
McAdam, John Lodon, 31, 32, 33, 151
Meade, Dr William, 150
Melbourne, Lord, 133, 166
Mellon, Harriett, 177
Meux, Sir Henry Bruce, 126
Milestones, 33
Milling industry, 210
Mills, Peter, 125
Mimms, South, 91, 155
Mimram, river 38, 46, 84, 198
More, Sir John, 122
Morris, William, 146, 162, 166
Morrison, Sir Richard, 157
Mortain, Robert, Count of, 83
Mosquito aircraft, 126
Mounteagle, Lord, 101, 130
Mount, Stephen, Lord, 133
Munden, Great and Little, 61, 106
Myddleton, Sir Hugh, 201
Mylne family, 151
Mymms, North, 113, 152

N

New River, 151, 201-3
New Towns, 15, 16
Newce, Clement and William, 148
Newnham, 20, 74
Nollekens, Joseph, 162
No Mans Land Common, 124, 161
Norden, John, 30, 168
Northaw, 77, 152
Northcliffe, Lord, 192
Northchurch, 68, 160, 194
Northwood (Middx), 37
Nowell, Rev. Alexander, 148

O

O'Connor, Fergus, 195
Offley, 27, 63, 162
Oldaker, Henry and Robert, 191
Oman, Carola, 112

P

Page, John, 194
Palmerston, Lord, 133, 166
Papermaking industry, 212

Index

Park Street, 56, 183
Parsley, John, 124
Paumier, Pierre, 214
Pelham, Furneux, 102, 130, 146, 210; Stocking, 195
Penefather, Edward, 196
Pepys, Samuel, 109, 164, 170, 181, 182
Perient, John, 164; **218**
Peter the Wild Boy, 160
Pevsner, Sir Nikolaus, 74, 103, 107, 108, 120, 130, 138, 150, 161, 162
Pickford, Thomas, 191
Pirton, 22, 68, 95
Plumer, Walter, 127
Pope, Alexander, 121
Posting Boxes, 216
Potters Bar, 34, 37, 174
Pre-history, 40-57
Preston, 74, 162
Probert, William, 183
Puckeridge, 33, 52, 181, 200
Pulham, James, 93
Pym, Rev. Edmund, 143

Q

Quin, river, 43

R

Radlett, 37
Railways, 37, 197-200
Ransom, John, 216
Raven, John, 160
Raymond, Sir Robert, 125
Reading (Berks), 32
Redbourn, 46, 47, 62, 68, 161, 188, 215
Reed, 19, 27, 77, 95, 106, 145, 210; **36**
Revett, Nicholas, 165
Rhodes, Rev. Francis, 149
Rib, river, 43, 54
Richard II, 98
Rickmansworth, 32, 34, 37, 56, 121, 157, 195, 197, 203, 212, 214; **81**
Ridge, 195
Roads, 21-39
Robinson, Henry Crabb, 182
Robinson, William, 114
Rookwood, Ambrose, 191

Rothschild, Lionel Nathan de, 123, 194; Lionel Walter, 2nd Baron, 123
Rumbold, Richard, 104
Rumbold, Sir Thomas, 129
Rushden, 130
Rye House, 104; **65**

S

Sadleir, Sir Ralph, 129, 147; Sir Thomas, 147
Saffron Walden (Essex), 91
St Albans (City, Abbey and Abbots), 20, 27-30, 33, 34, 45, 50, 62-4, 79, 116, 122, 125, 134-42, 184-8, 195, 197, 200, 211, 212, 214; **60, 118, 135, 154**
St Clare, Hamo de, 93
St Ippolletts, 176
Salisbury, Lords (Cecil), 32, 85, 101, 107-13, 126, 166, 212; 'Gout Track' (A 414, A 412, A 404), 32
Salusbury, Sir Robert, 162
Sandon, 43, 77, 95
Sandridge, 133
Sarratt, 20, 56, 62, 158; **136**
Sawbridgeworth, 20, 69, 106, 149, 177, 197, 206
Saye, Sir John, Sir William, 151
Scott, Sir George Gilbert, 140, 158
Scott, Sir Walter, 129
Sebright, Sir John, 124
Shaw, George Bernard, 165
Shenley, 125, 155, 195
Silk industry, 16, 214
Smith, Rev. John, 143
Smith, Samuel, 124
Snow, Sir Jeremiah, 126
Soane, Lord John, 124
Somers, Lord John, 122, 155
Spellbrook, 178
Standon, 72, 129, 146, 181, 211, 212; **136, 171**
Stanstead Abbots, 69, 104, 149, 195, 206; **136**
Stevenage, 16, 19, 20, 23, 27, 43, 62, 162, 174, 198
Stephens, Dr Henry, 191
Stirling, Edward, 180
Stony, Andrew Robinson, 132
Stort, river, 33, 127, 201, 205
Strange, Rev. Alexander, 146

Street, G. E., 155
Styles, Benjamin Hoskin, 121
Sullivan, Sir Arthur, 132

T

Taylor, John, 'Water poet', 31, 168
Taylor, Sir Robert, 116, 125
Teale, William, 104
Telford, Thomas, 31
Temple Bar, 126
Tewin, 24, 57, 127, 128
Thackeray, Rev. Francis, 152
Therfield, 77, 95, 106, 145
Thorley, 123
Throcking, 62
'Thumb, General Tom', 186
Thundridge, 62
Thurtell, John, 183
Tidcombe, George, 212
Tittenhanger, 125
Toll-houses, 34
Tonwell, 34, 211
Tradescant, John, 108
Tree, Ellen, 180
Tring, 19, 22, 23, 38, 62, 72, 123, 160, 194, 197, 203, 211, 215; **99**
Trusler, Rev. John, 150
Turpin, Dick, 174

V

Valognes, Peter de, 92
Ver, river, 214
Verney, Sir Ralph, 161
Verulam, Earl, 116
Verulamium, 23, 27, 48-52; **25**
Victoria, Queen, 194

W

Wadesmill, 37, 61, 181
Wakeley, 61

Walden, King's, 162, 210; St Paul's (and Whitwell), 62, 132, 162, 195, 196; **117**
Walkern, 93
Walpole, Horace, 128; Sir Robert, 112
Waltham Cross, 105, 178
Walton, Isaak, 148, 179
Wangford, Benjamin, 157
Ware, 16, 23, 27, 29, 68, 69, 105, 149, 180, 206, 209; **207**
Washington, George, 161
Watford, 16, 20, 23, 32, 37, 38, 56, 68, 72, 122, 125, 169, 192, 197, 199, 200, 201, 212, 214
Watling Street (A 5), 23, 43, 52
Watton-at-Stone, 69, 128, 195, 196
Watts, Dr Isaac, 126
Weare, William, 183
Wellington, Duke of, 129
Welwyn, 23, 24, 29, 46, 55, 68, 164, 169, 170, 198
Welwyn Garden City, 56, 198
Westmacott, Sir Richard, 158
Westmill, 27, 74; **42**
Weston, 77, 210
Wheathampstead, 22, 46, 161, 191
Wheeler, Sir Mortimer, 46, 50
Wheeler, Rosina, 115
Whitney, 'Captain' James, 179
Whittingham, Sir Robert, 161
Whittington, Amelia Hinde, 164
Widford, 43, 127, 196
Wigginton, 194
William of Normandy (William I), 83, 84
Wilkes, John, 85
Woollam, John, 214
Woolmer Green, 164
Wormley, 37
Worsley, John, 85
Wren, Sir Christopher, 123
Wyatt, James, 119
Wyatville, Sir Jeffrey, 119, 159
Wymondley, Great, 93, 163; Little, 195

Y

Young, Dr Edward, 164